BUSINESS CARD GRAPHICS

ROCKPORT PUBLISHERS · ROCKPORT, MASSACHUSETTS
Distributed by North Light Books · Cincinnati, Ohio
P·I·E BOOKS

BUSINESS CARD GRAPHICS

First published in North and South America by:
Rockport Publishers, Inc.
P.O. Box 396
Five Smith Street
Rockport, Massachusetts 01966
Telephone: (508) 546-9590
Fax: (508) 546-7141
Telex: 5106019284 ROCKORT PUB

Distributed to the book trade and art trade in the U.S.
and Canada by:
North Light, an imprint of
F & W Publications
1507 Dana Avenue
Cincinnati, Ohio 45207
Telephone: (513) 531-2222

ISBN 1-56496-012-9

10 9 8 7 6 5 4 3 2 1

Printed in Japan

ビジネスカード グラフィックス

P·I·E BOOKS

はじめに

　今日、私達を取囲む情報伝達手段は実に多種多様化を極めている。放送、通信、出版等の組織力による情報網が大発展を遂げる一方で、手紙や電話、口コミ等、きわめて個人的な情報網の重要性も私達は日常生活の中で、十分認識している。今回ここに採り上げた〝名刺〟も個人間でやりとりされる大切な情報交換である。にもかかわらず多くの名刺群は受け取った時こそ丁重に取扱われても、一読してしまえば、後は必要な時までほとんど顧みられずにいるのが実状ではないだろうか。印象に残る名刺が少ないせいもある。名刺交換があまりにも日常的すぎてそこに特別な価値を感じにくいのかもしれない。しかし名刺は挨拶代わりとも言われるように、紙面による挨拶でもある。しかも日常会話のように時とともに都合よく消えていってはくれない。反面、手紙ほどの親密さは持たず、飾るほど大きくもない。あっさり破り捨てるのには忍びない。要するに公的紙面のようでいて私的書面でもある。使い捨て用品のようでいて資料としての役割も果たす。ここに名刺の持つ実に特異な一面が見いだされはしないだろうか。

　では、このわずか90㎜×50㎜の小さな紙片に敢えて目を凝らしてみよう。すると、小さいからこそ緻密なデザインを生

みだしていること、また形、大きさ、色等の選択、文字や書体、ロゴタイプ、イラストレーション等の組み合わせが思いのほか様々な表情を創り出している事に気づかされる。なかにはその個人、その法人の自己主張を強く感じさせるものや、気質さえ垣間見させてくれるものに出逢うこともある。ひとつの文字、ひとつのレイアウトへのこだわりが、私達の視覚に訴え、微妙に奥深く心を揺り動かす。また、必要事項と独創的なデザインを違和感なく溶け合わせ、奇をてらうのでもなく、名刺としての役割を果たすことを第一義的に考えた、礼儀正しさが滲み出ているものからは、その本人の持つ際立った感性を読みとることさえできる。

　瞬時にして印象を刻み込まれる可能性が高いからこそ、単なる紙切れで終わらせない為のテクニック、いかにして細かい配慮を施したらよいのかという一種 "デザインの哲学" とでも呼ぶべき創造性を味わえるかもしれないところに、名刺だけが持つ謙虚で律儀な醍醐味があると言えよう。

　最後に、この本の出版にあたり、作品の提供をしてくださった方々に心から感謝したい。

ピエ・ブックス編集部

Introduction

The methods of communicating information in today's society are extremely diverse. Broadcasting and print media organizations have created a broad-based information network, while letters, the telephone and word of mouth form a very personal one.

The business cards shown here are also an important form of information exchange between individuals. The majority of business cards, however, are received as a matter of courtesy, glanced over and usually ignored until needed later for reference. This may reflect the scarcity of impression-making cards or the act of exchanging cards has become so commonplace that the card itself is overlooked.

It is said that business cards are a substitute for greetings. Unlike the ephemeral spoken word, they are tangible greetings. While business cards lack the intimacy of a letter and are too small to display, they are disposable data that is not so readily thrown away. In short, business cards have both a public and private function.

When we study this 50×90mm piece of paper, we see that because of its scale, the design is subtly intricate. Through thoughtful use of format, size, color, typography and typeface, logomark and illustration, the designer can express an endless variety of messages. Amoung these, the self-image of the individual or corporation is primary and their sensibility alluded to. Visual appeal and the ability to evoke emotion stems from scrutinizing the form and position of every element. Content and image must create a single, harmonious statement. A successful business card is not only a display of original design, but above all must fulfil its role as a communication piece. Beneath the formality we should sense the individual.

Because impressions are formed in an instant, what makes a card distinct from just another scrap of paper is a design philosophy that combines scrupulous attention to detail with a creativity that expresses the business card's unique modesty, integrity and charm.

We would like to express our gratitude to the many designers who have made their work available for this publication.

THE EDITORIAL STAFF OF P·I·E BOOKS.

Editorial Notes

This book is a collection of
1200 business cards carefully
selected from 5000
cards representing a
wide variety of business
categories and graphic styles.
The editorial policy upon
which selection was determined
emphasized the visual
aspects of the design.
Information about each piece
is indicated as follows:

CD: Creative Director
AD: Art Director
D: Designer
I: Illustrator
P: Photographer
CW: Copywriter
A: Artist
T: Typographer
C: Calligrapher
CI: C.I.Designer
DF: Design Firm

アート・ギャラリー
STUDIO FURNIQUE
Art Gallery
AD:Dean Morris
DF:Stylism

Grafik-Design · Konzeption · Illustration
Audiovisuelle Medien · Mendelssohnstr. 42
6000 Frankfurt am Main · Telefon 749413

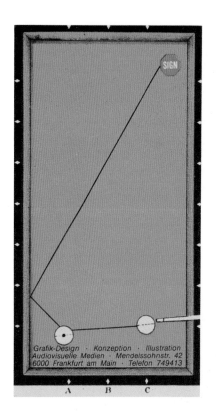

Grafik-Design · Konzeption · Illustration
Audiovisuelle Medien · Mendelssohnstr. 42
6000 Frankfurt am Main · Telefon 749413

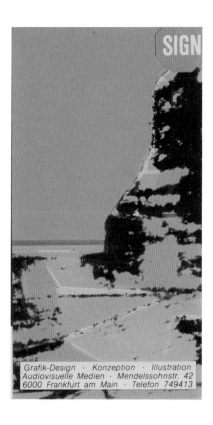

Grafik-Design · Konzeption · Illustration
Audiovisuelle Medien · Mendelssohnstr. 42
6000 Frankfurt am Main · Telefon 749413

Grafik-Design · Konzeption · Illustration
Audiovisuelle Medien · Mendelssohnstr. 42
6000 Frankfurt am Main · Telefon 749413

Grafik-Design · Konzeption · Illustration
Audiovisuelle Medien · Mendelssohnstr. 42
6000 Frankfurt am Main · Telefon 749413

Grafik-Design
Mendelssohnstr. 42 · Konzeption · 6000 Frankfurt am Main · Illustration · Audiovisuelle Medien · Telefon 749413

デザイン
STUDIO SIGN
Design
AD, D:Karl W. Henschel
I:H. Jung
DF:Studio Sign

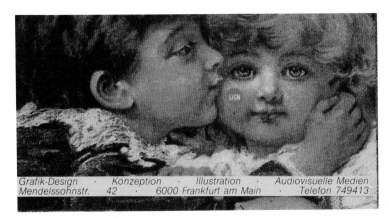

Grafik-Design · Konzeption · Illustration · Audiovisuelle Medien
Mendelssohnstr. 42 · 6000 Frankfurt am Main · Telefon 749413

Grafik-Design · Konzeption · Illustration ·
Audiovisuelle Medien · Mendelssohnstr. 42 ·
6000 Frankfurt am Main · Telefon 749413

Grafik-Design · Konzeption · Illustration ·
Audiovisuelle Medien · Mendelssohnstr. 42 ·
6000 Frankfurt am Main · Telefon 749413

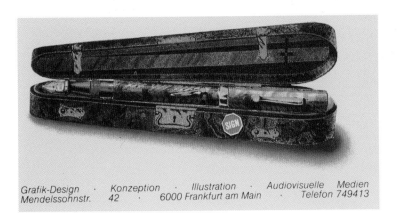

Grafik-Design · Konzeption · Illustration · Audiovisuelle Medien
Mendelssohnstr. 42 · 6000 Frankfurt am Main · Telefon 749413

Grafik-Design · Konzeption · Illustration ·
Audiovisuelle Medien · Mendelssohnstr. 42 ·
6000 Frankfurt am Main · Telefon 749413

11

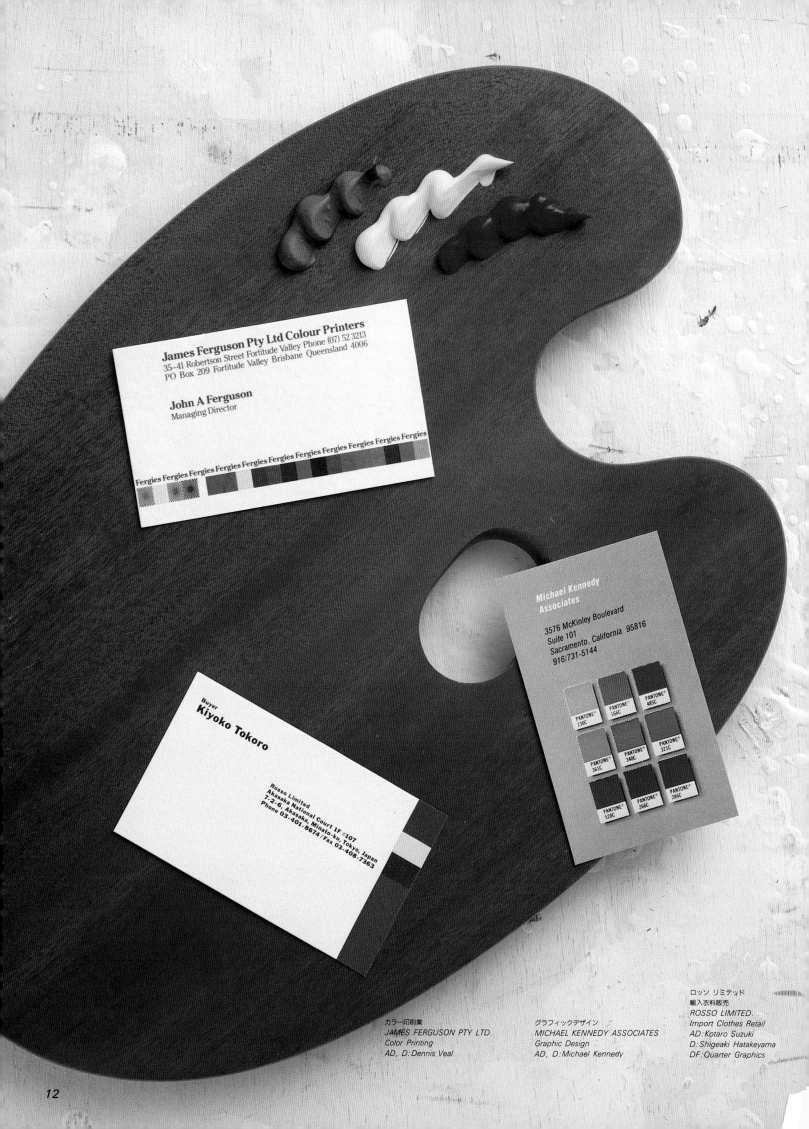

James Ferguson Pty Ltd Colour Printers
35–41 Robertson Street Fortitude Valley Phone (07) 52 3213
PO Box 209 Fortitude Valley Brisbane Queensland 4006

John A Ferguson
Managing Director

Fergies Fergies Fergies Fergies Fergies Fergies Fergies Fergies Fergies Fergies

**Michael Kennedy
Associates**

3576 McKinley Boulevard
Suite 101
Sacramento, California 95816
916/731-5144

Buyer
Kiyoko Tokoro

Rosso Limited
Akasaka National Court 1F =107
7-2-6, Akasaka, Minato-ku, Tokyo, Japan
Phone 03-401-8674/Fax 03-408-7363

カラー印刷業
JAMES FERGUSON PTY LTD.
Color Printing
AD, D:Dennis Veal

グラフィックデザイン
MICHAEL KENNEDY ASSOCIATES
Graphic Design
AD, D:Michael Kennedy

ロッソ リミテッド
輸入衣料販売
ROSSO LIMITED.
Import Clothes Retail
AD:Kotaro Suzuki
D:Shigeaki Hatakeyama
DF:Quarter Graphics

ライター/放送プロデューサー
Ellie Mac Dougall
Writer / Broadcast Producer
AD, D:Appleton Design
P:Frank Marchese

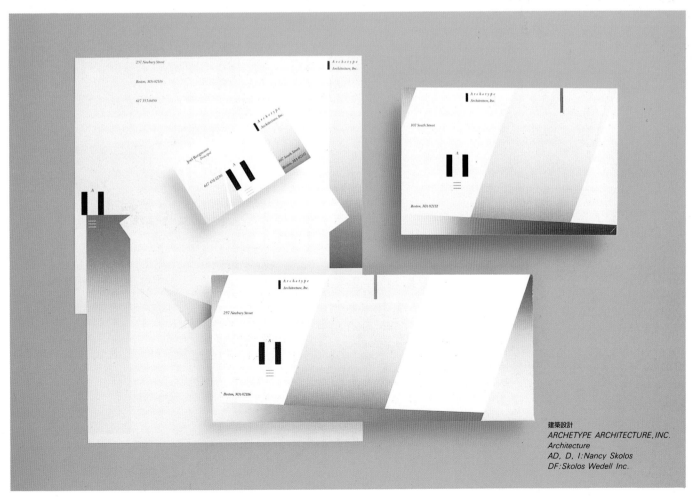

建築設計
ARCHETYPE ARCHITECTURE, INC.
Architecture
AD, D, I:Nancy Skolos
DF:Skolos Wedell Inc.

INSIGHTFUL POWER OF
OBSERVATION OF SPECIALIST

FABULOUS PRODUCTION
FOR TRANSMITTING
THE EMOTION

株式会社 イフカンパニー
代表取締役
日本パッケージデザイン協会会員
高 橋 敏
〒107 東京都港区南青山7-4-2アトリウム青山2D
TEL 03(406)0731 (代) FAX 03(406)0738

ART DIRECTOR
VING TAKAHASHI
IFF COMPANY INC.

ATRIUM AOYAMA2D, 7-4-2, MINAMI-AOYAMA,
MINATO-KU, TOKYO, JAPAN
PHONE : 03-406-0731

㈱イフカンパニー
パッケージ・グラフィック・デザイン
IFF COMPANY INC
Package Graphics Design
AD:Vin Takahashi
D:Masakazu Tagawa

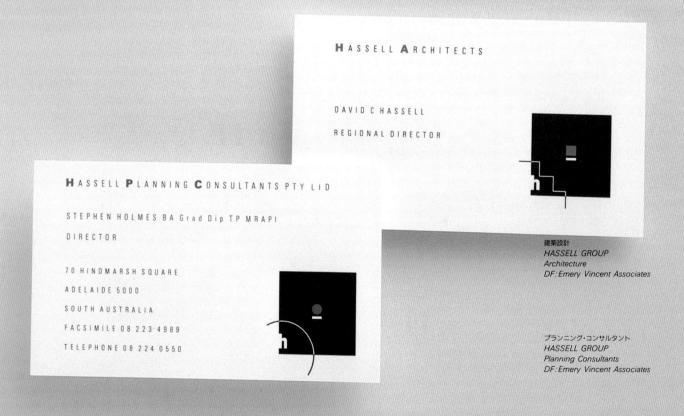

建築設計
HASSELL GROUP
Architecture
DF:Emery Vincent Associates

プランニング・コンサルタント
HASSELL GROUP
Planning Consultants
DF:Emery Vincent Associates

企画会社
MARKS COMMUNICATION INC.
Communications
AD, D:Rod Dyer
DF:Rod Dyer Group, Inc.

調査
MARCO
Research
AD, D, I:Eric Jon Read

グラフィックデザイン
READ & ASSOCIATES
Graphic Design
AD, D, I:Eric Jon Read

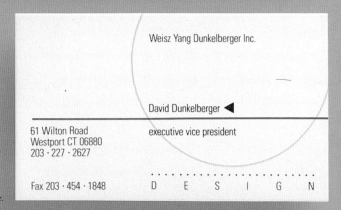

グラフィックデザイン
WYD
Graphic Design
AD, D:Larry Yang
DF:Weisz Yang Dunkelberger Inc.

建築設計
MONIGHAM+ASSOCIATES
Architecture
AD:Michael Dunlavey
D:Kevin Yee

JANIS
BOEHM
DESIGN

TRACY GIBBONS
DESIGNER

717 SOUTH WELLS STREET
CHICAGO, ILLINOIS 60607
312.427.7400

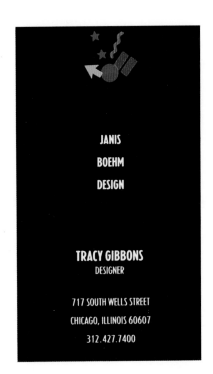

JANIS
BOEHM
DESIGN

TRACY GIBBONS
DESIGNER

717 SOUTH WELLS STREET
CHICAGO, ILLINOIS 60607
312.427.7400

JANIS
BOEHM
DESIGN

JANIS BOEHM
PRINCIPAL

717 SOUTH WELLS STREET
CHICAGO, ILLINOIS 60607
312.427.7400

JANIS
BOEHM
DESIGN

JANIS BOEHM
PRINCIPAL

717 SOUTH WELLS STREET
CHICAGO, ILLINOIS 60607
312.427.7400

グラフィックデザイン
JANIS BOEHM DESIGN
Graphic Design
AD, D:Janis Boehm
DF:Janis Boehm Design

青年慈善団体
FRESH FORCE
Youth Volunteer Organization
AD, D, I:Charles Spencer Anderson
DF:Charles S.Anderson Design Co.

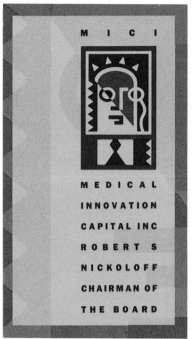

医療産業の投下資本グループ
MICI
Venture Capital Group for the Medical Industry
AD, D, I:Charles Spencer Anderson
DF:Charles S.Anderson Design Co.

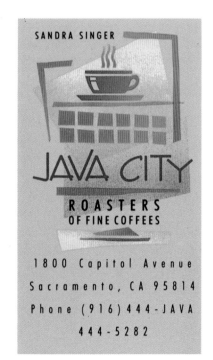

コーヒー豆製造販売
JAVA CITY
Retail/Wholesale Coffee Roaster
AD:Michael Dunlavey
D:Lindy Dunlavey
DF:The Dunlavey Studio

アイスクリーム・パーラー
DELICKTABLES
Ice Cream Parlor
AD, D, I:Valerie Wong
DF:The Design Office of Wong & Yeo

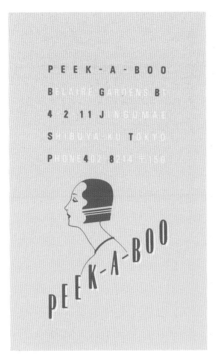

ピーク・ア・ブー
美容室
PEEK-A-BOO
Hair Salon
AD:Naohisa Tsuchiya

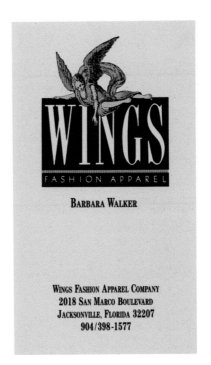

アパレルメーカー
WINGS FASHIONS
Apparel Maker
AD, I:Tom Schifanella
D:Tom Nuijens
DF:Robin Shepherd Studios

デリカテッセン
OZZIE'S DELI
Delicatessen
AD, D, I:Valerie Wong
DF:The Design Office of Wong & Yeo

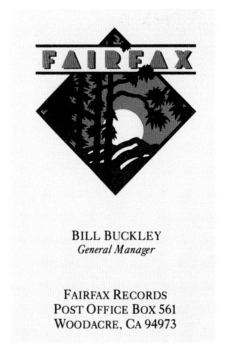

レコード会社
FAIRFAX RECORDS
Record Company
AD:Ross Carron
D:Lance Anderson
DF:Carron Design

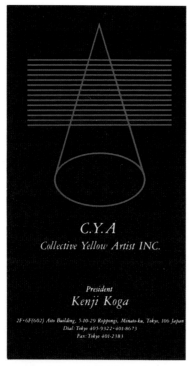

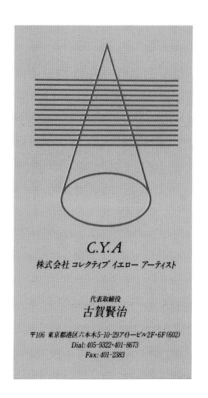

㈱コレクティブ イエロー アーティスト
広告企画/制作
COLLECTIVE YELLOW ARTIST INC.
Advertising
AD:Kenji Koga

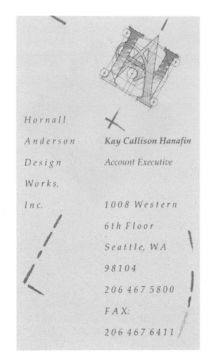

デザイン
HORNALL ANDERSON DESIGN WORKS
Design
AD, D:Jack Anderson
DF:Hornall Anderson Design Works

ゴールド
ディスコ
GOLD
Discotheque
AD, D:Koichi Yoshida

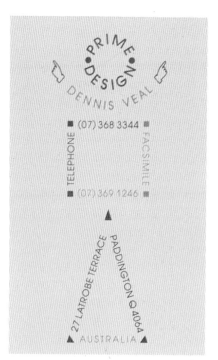

旅行代理店
TRAVEL ASSOCIATES INC.
Travel Agency
AD, D, I:Debbie Hahn
DF:Playne Design

グラフィックデザイン
PRIME DESIGN
Graphic Design
AD, D:Dennis Veal
I:Monica-Krueger

衣料品店
WOOLIES
Clothing Store
AD:Ross Carron
D:Joanne Maass
DF:Carron Design

建築物検査会社
GCIS
Building Inspection
AD, D, I:Bruce Yelaska
DF:Bruce Yelaska Design

ICHIRO MURAYAMA
PRESIDENT

SEIWA CORPORATION
1-1-1 SHIMOOCHIAI SHINJUKU-KU
TOKYO 161 JAPAN
TELEPHONE 03-364-2111
FAX 03-371-0638

㈱セイワ
染色メーカー/染色学校/総合ファションビル
SEIWA CORPORATION
Dye Manufacture & School/Fashion Center
AD, D:Hiromi Inayoshi

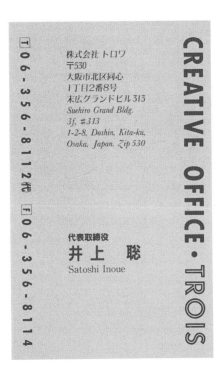

株式会社 トロワ
〒530
大阪市北区同心
1丁目2番8号
末広グランドビル313
Suehiro Grand Bldg.
3f, #313
1-2-8, Doshin, Kita-ku,
Osaka, Japan. Zip 530

代表取締役
井上 聡
Satoshi Inoue

㈱トロワ
イベント企画
CREATIVE OFFICE TROIS
Event Planning
AD, D:Hirofumi Tsuchitani
DF:Studio Idea

代表取締役
中村文人

株式会社 FNクリエイティヴ
〒176東京都練馬区高松1-38-29
TEL 03-999-9497 FAX 03-825-1136

㈱FNクリエイティヴ
企画/広告
FUTURE NETWORK CREATIVE INC.
Planning/Advertising
AD:Hiroki Taniguchi
D:Ichiro Tanida

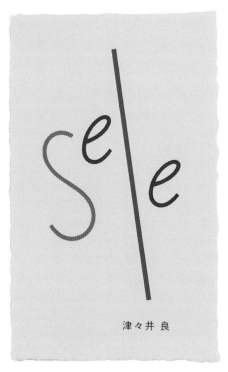

津々井 良

セレ
シルクスクリーン工房
SELE
Silk Screen Studio
AD, D:Hiromi Inayoshi

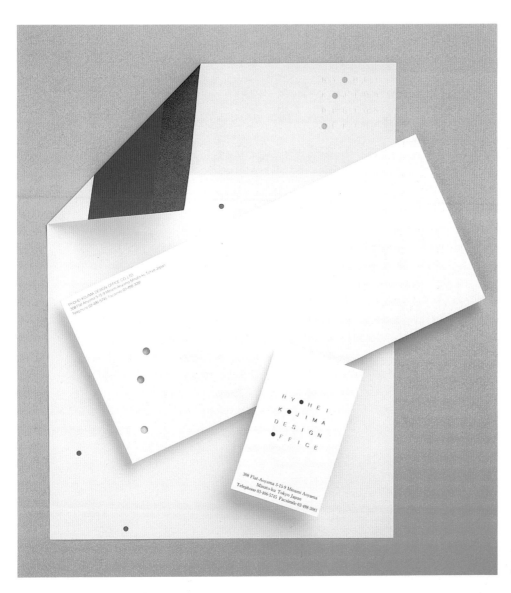

小島良平デザイン事務所
グラフィックデザイン
RYOHEI KOJIMA DESIGN OFFICE
Graphic Design
AD, D:Ryohei Kojima

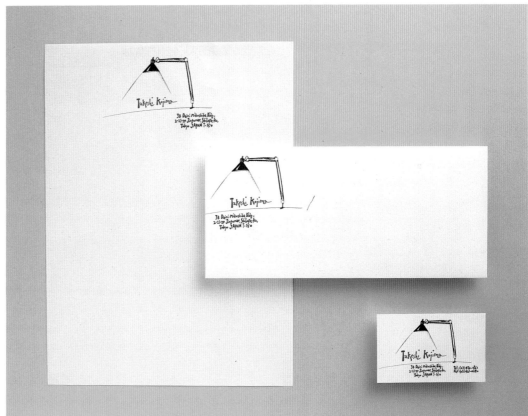

小島　武
イラストレーション/グラフィックデザイン
TAKESHI KOJIMA
Illustration/Graphic Design
AD, D, I:Takeshi Kojima

TOKIデザイン室
デザイン
TOKI DESIGN STUDIO
Design
AD, D:Tokiyoshi Tsubouchi
青山見本帖より

アルゾ㈱
アパレルの企画製造/販売
ALZO
Apparel Manufacture/Sales
AD, D:Toshihiro Onimaru

OSAMA
SCRITTURA
SPA

Armando Tschang
Chief executive officer

株式会社アイム 〒150東京都渋谷区南平台町13-4 308 電話03(770)5961

PREMONT・SNC

石田正実

MUSTARD 〒107 東京都港区南青山4-8-4 パレス南青山501
TEL. 03(423)4748 FAX. 03(423)4749

日本雑貨の輸入
OSAMA SCRITTURA
Japanese Goods Importer
AD, D: Vittorio Prina
DF: Visual Due

㈱アイム
広告企画/制作
I'M CO., LTD.
Advertising
AD: Yukio Ikoma
D: Yumiko Kawasaki
T: Katsumi Asaba

製版会社
PREMONT
Color Separation
AD, D: Vittorio Prina
DF: Visual Due

マスタード
広告/編集
MUSTARD LTD.
Advertising/Editing
D: Masami Shimada

池田源英
イラストレーション/デザイン
GEN·EI IKEDA
Illustration/Graphic Design
D:Gen·El Ikeda

嘉瑞工房
欧文活版印刷
THE KAZUI PRESS LTD
Letterpress Printing
D:Juzo Takaoka

うちの順子
イラストレーション
JUNKO UCHINO
Illustration
AD, D, I:Junko Uchino

南川　直
麻雀屋
TADASHI MINAMIKAWA
Mah-Jong Parlour
D:Tadashi Minamikawa

樋口雅山房
書道家
GAZANBO HIGUCHI
Calligrapher
C:Gazanbo Higuchi

もぐら庵
遊印家
MOGURA AN
Seal Carver
AD, D: Koji Ikeda

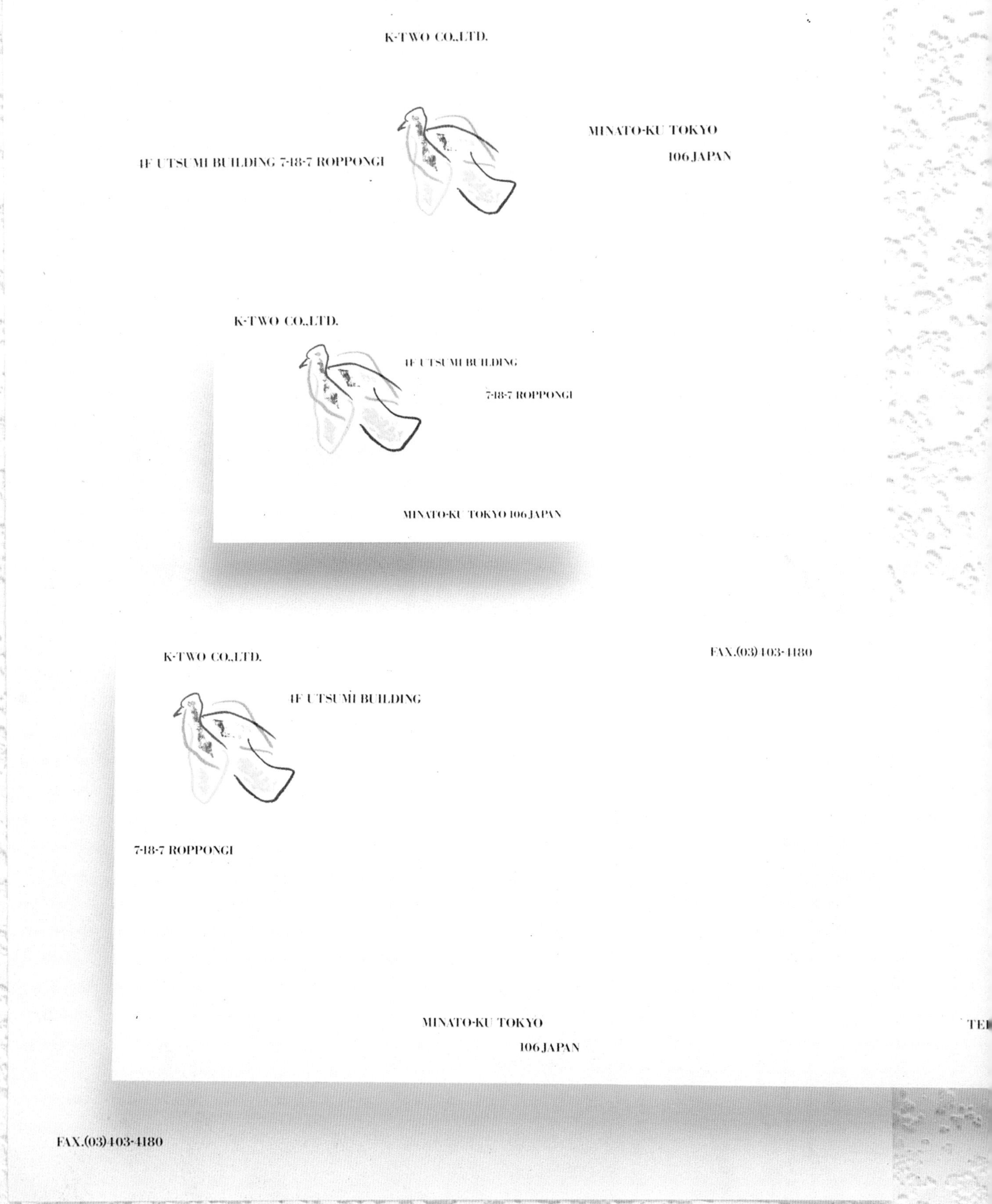

K-TWO CO.,LTD.

1F UTSUMI BUILDING 7-18-7 ROPPONGI

MINATO-KU TOKYO

106 JAPAN

K-TWO CO.,LTD.

1F UTSUMI BUILDING

7-18-7 ROPPONGI

MINATO-KU TOKYO 106 JAPAN

K-TWO CO.,LTD.

1F UTSUMI BUILDING

FAX.(03)403-4180

7-18-7 ROPPONGI

MINATO-KU TOKYO

106 JAPAN

TEI

FAX.(03)403-4180

ケーツー
デザイン
K₂
Design
D:Keisuke Nagatomo

30

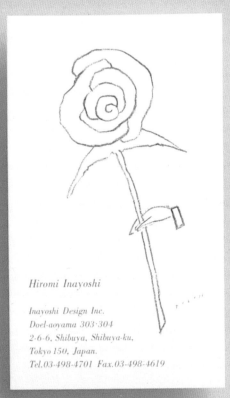

Hiromi Inayoshi

Inayoshi Design Inc.
Doel-aoyama 303-304
2-6-6, Shibuya, Shibuya-ku,
Tokyo 150, Japan.
Tel.03-498-4701 Fax.03-498-4619

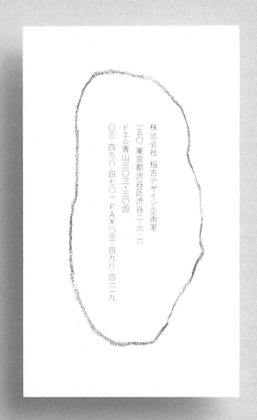

㈱稲吉デザイン
グラフィックデザイン
INAYOSHI DESING INC.
Graphic Design
AD, D:Hiromi Inayoshi
I:Jean-Michel Folon

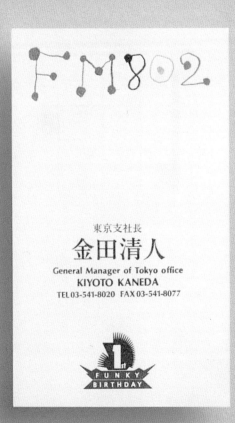

東京支社長
金田清人
General Manager of Tokyo office
KIYOTO KANEDA
TEL 03-541-8020 FAX 03-541-8077

㈱FM802
ラジオ放送局
FM802 CO.,LTD.
Radio Station
AD, D:Keisuke Nagatomo
I:Seitaro Kuroda

㈱FM802
ラジオ放送局
FM802 CO.,LTD.
Radio Station
AD, D:Keisuke Nagatomo
I:Seitaro Kuroda

Hiroshi Inayoshi

President

WORK BRAIN

Work Brain Inc.
Nishi Shinjuku KB Plaza 1002
6-11-3 Nishi Shinjuku
Shinjuku-ku Tokyo 160 Japan
Phone 03 346 3342
Fax 03 346 3394

ワークブレイン㈱
経営コンサルタント
WORK BRAIN INC.
Management Consulting
AD, D:Hiromi Inayoshi
I:Jean-Michel Folon

TSUKASA HASEGAWA

J CLUB KASUMIGAURA COURSE

6-8-17 ROPPONGI MINATO-KU

TOKYO 106 JAPAN

TELEPHONE 03-470-6270

Jクラブ霞ヶ浦コース
ゴルフコース
J-CLUB KASUMIGAURA COURSE
Golf Course
AD, D:Hiromi Inayoshi
I:Jean-Michel Folon

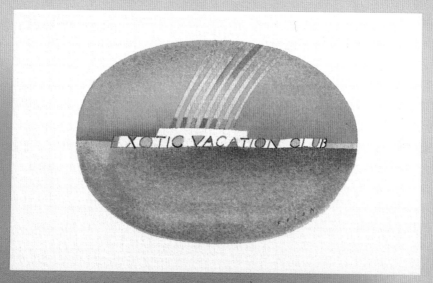

エキゾチックバケーション クラブ
旅行代理店
EXOTIC VACATION CLUB
Travel Agency
AD, D:Hiromi Inayoshi
I:Jean-Michel Folon

Shin Matsunaga

PEACE Corporation
8th Floor, Ishibashi-kogyo Bldg.,
7-3-1, Minami-Aoyama, Minato-ku, Tokyo, 107 Japan
Tel: 499-0291,0292 Fax: 499-3309

PEACE Corporation
8th Floor, Ishibashi-kogyo Bldg.,
7-3-1, Minami-Aoyama, Minato-ku, Tokyo, 107 Japan
Tel: 499-0291,0292 Fax: 499-3309

PEACE Corporation
8th Floor, Ishibashi-kogyo Bldg.,
7-3-1, Minami-Aoyama, Minato-ku, Tokyo, 107 Japan
Tel: 499-0291,0292 Fax: 499-3309

㈱松永真デザイン事務所
デザイン
SHIN MATSUNAGA DESIGN INC.
Design
AD, D: Shin Matsunaga
青山見本帖より

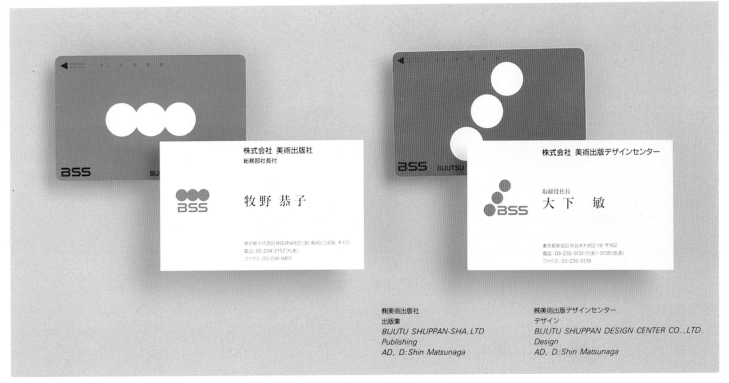

株式会社 美術出版社
総務部社長付

牧野 恭子

東京都千代田区神田神保町2-36 柏岡ビル6階 〒101
電話: 03-234-2157 (代表)
ファクス: 03-234-9451

株式会社 美術出版デザインセンター

取締役社長
大下 敏

東京都新宿区市谷本村町2-19 〒162
電話: 03-235-5131 (代表) -5138 (直通)
ファクス: 03-235-5139

㈱美術出版社
出版業
BIJUTU SHUPPAN-SHA, LTD
Publishing
AD, D: Shin Matsunaga

㈱美術出版デザインセンター
デザイン
BIJUTU SHUPPAN DESIGN CENTER CO., LTD.
Design
AD, D: Shin Matsunaga

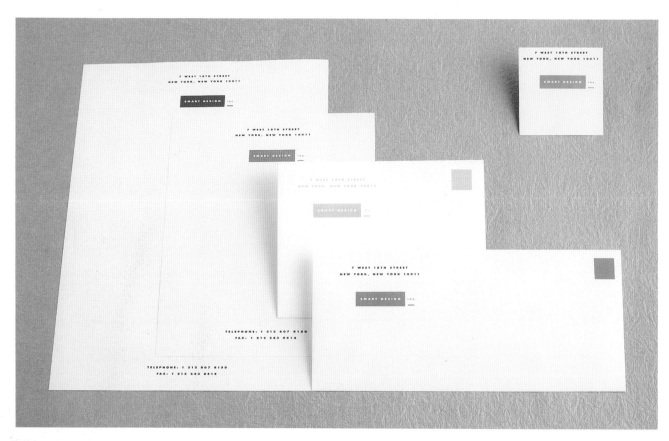

デザイン
SMART DESIGN
Design
AD, D:Debbie Hahn
DF:Smart Design

㈱トゥモローランド
ファッション企画/製造販売
TOMORROWLAND CO.,LTD.
Fashion Planning/Manufacture/Sales
AD:Tamotsu Yagi
D:Wakako Tsuchiya

宮本武人デザイン事務所
デザイン
MIYAMOTO TAKETO DESIGN OFFICE
Design
AD, D:Taketo Miyamoto

35

ソフトウエアー
ASYMETRIX CORPORATION
Software
AD, D:Jack Anderson
D:Greg walters
C:Bruce Hale
DF:Hornall Anderson Design Works

建築設計
CARSON FERRIN ARCHITECTS
Architecture
AD, D:Jack Anderson
P:Greg Krogstag
DF:Hornall Anderson Design Works

グラフィックデザイン
KIRK GELARDI DESIGN
Graphic Design
AD, D, I:Eric Jon Read

インテリア・デザイン
TRAINOR & ASSOCIATES
Interior Design
AD:Michael Dunlavey
D:Heidi tomlinson
DF:The Dunlavey Studio

デザイン/写真
SKOLOS WEDELL+RAYNOR
Design/Photography
AD, D, I:Nancy Skolos
DF:Skolos Wedell Inc.

写真
RALSTON PHOTOGRAPHY
Photography
AD, D:Jack Anderson
D, I:Cheri Huber
DF:Hornall Anderson Design Works

グラフィックデザイン
WILKINS & PETERSON
Graphic Design
AD, D:Warren Wilkins
AD, D:Tommer Peterson
DF:Wilkins & Peterson

ビデオ制作
RAIMONDI FILMS
Video Film Production
AD, D, I:James W.Keaton
DF:GK＋D Communications Inc.

デザイン
BRS WATANO
Design
AD, D:Shigeru Watano

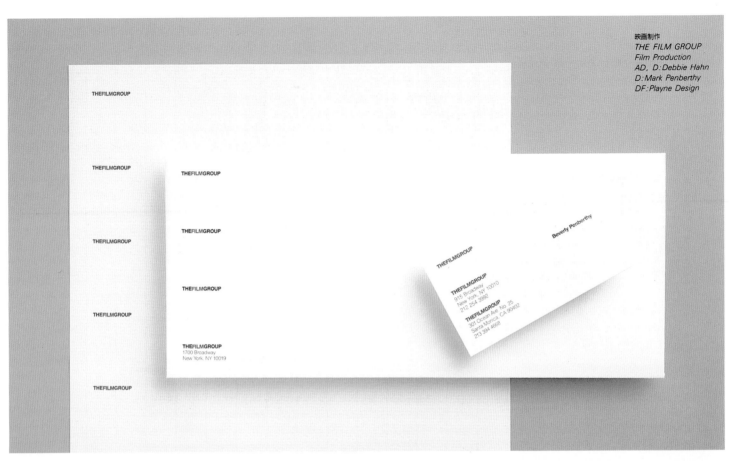

映画制作
THE FILM GROUP
Film Production
AD, D:Debbie Hahn
D:Mark Penberthy
DF:Playne Design

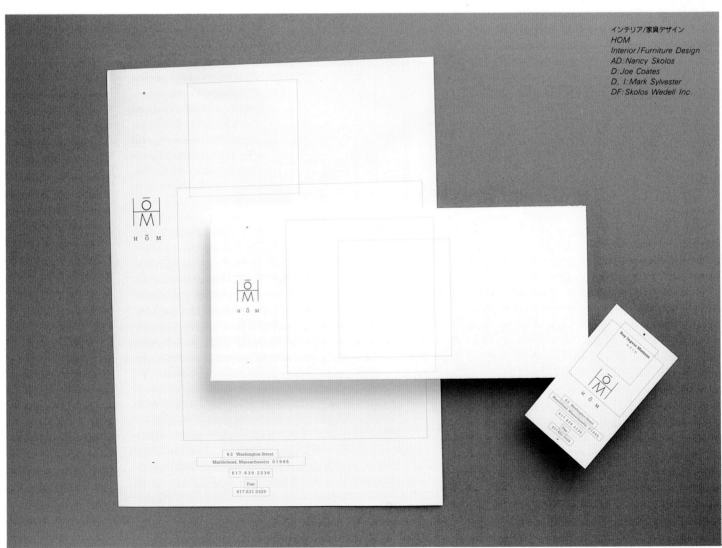

インテリア/家具デザイン
HOM
Interior /Furniture Design
AD:Nancy Skolos
D:Joe Coates
D, I:Mark Sylvester
DF:Skolos Wedell Inc.

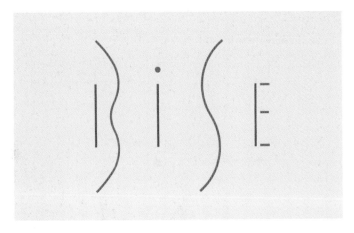

株式ビセ
イラストレーション/デザイン
BISE INC.
Illustration/Design
AD, D:Hiromi Inayoshi

グラフィックデザイン
TIM HARTFORD
Graphic Design
AD, D:Tim Hartford

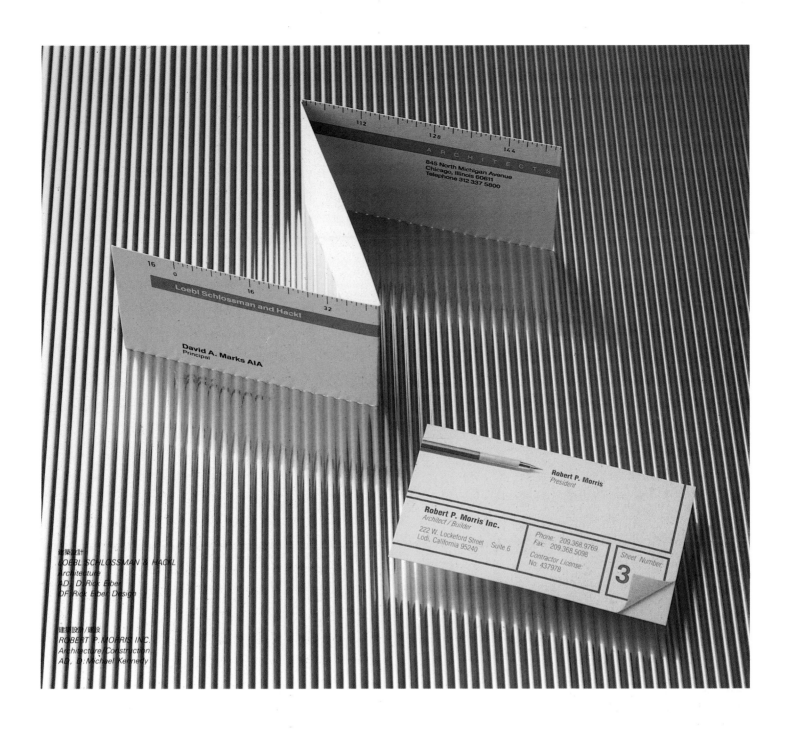

建築設計/
LOEBL SCHLOSSMAN & HACKL
Architecture
AD, D:Rick Eiber
DF:Rick Eiber Design

建築設計/建設
ROBERT P. MORRIS INC.
Architecture/Construction
AD, D:Michael Kennedy

建築設計/プロジェクト・マネージメント
ARCON
Architecture/Project Management
DF:Emery Vincent Associates

協会
DEVELOPMENT SERVICES ASSOCIATES
Consortium
AD, D:Jack Anderson
D:Juliet Shen
D:Heidi Hatlestad
DF:Hornall Anderson Design Works

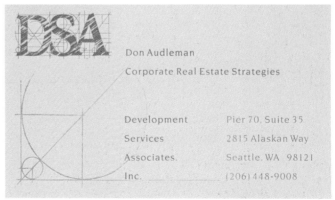

粂 万 里 子

DEBORA

デボラ／東京都港区南青山6-9-2日興児玉パレス南青山B-104 〒107 Tel.03-499-5937

㈱デボラ
靴の製造/小売
DEBORA CORPORATION
Shoe Manufacture/Retail
D:Akihiko Tsukamoto

O TETSUYA DESIGN STUDIO A

SUN MINAMI-AOYAMA 303   3-14-14, MINAMI-AOYAMA MINATO-KU TOKYO 107, JAPAN
TEL. 03-479-3697 FAX. 03-479-6434

太田徹也デザイン室
デザイン
TETSUYA OTA DESIGN STUDIO
Design
AD., D:Tetsuya Ota
青山見本帖より

Playne Design
96 Fort Greene Place
Brooklyn, NY 11217
718 834 8808

Debbie Hahn

佐 藤 富 太

〒150 東京都渋谷区代官山2-7シャトレ代官山301号
Tel. 03(760)1337 Fax. 03(760)1023

佐藤富太
ヘア・メイクアップ
TOMITA SATO
Hair/Make-up
AD. D:Sigenori Kameda

家具/グラフィック/工業デザイン
PLAYNE DESIGN
Furniture/Graphic/Industrial Design
AD., D., I:Debbie Hahn
DF:Playne Design

メイド・イン・ワールド
衣料品の販売
MADE IN WORLD
Clothing Sales
D:Hiroshi Ozawa

㈱ムーンラビット
デザイン
MOON RABBIT LTD.
Design
AD, D:Kotaro Hirano

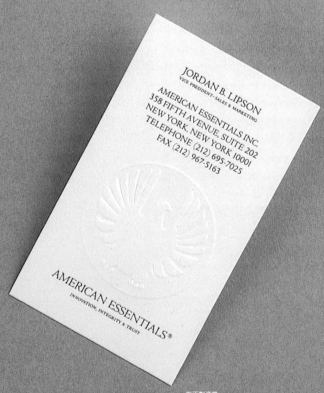

靴下製造業
AMERICAN ESSENTIALS
Hosiery Manufacture
AD, D, I:Raymond Lee
DF:Raymond & Associates LTD,Advertising

㈱スタジオホッパー
写真
STUDIO HOPPER
Photography
D:Syoji Ito

広報担当

福間祐子

アイムグループ
〒107 東京都港区南青山5-3-10 フロムファースト306
Phone:03-498-5251 Fax:03-498-5252

アイムグループ
アパレルメーカー
im GROUP
Apparel Maker
AD, D:Masaaki Hiromura
D:Toshiyuki Kojima
DF:Studio Ikks.

AXE COMPANY LIMITED

松井雅美
代表取締役

株式会社アクス
〒107 東京都港区南青山5-12-3 ヨネダビル4F　TEL.03-407-9067　FAX.03-498-0448
〒174 東京都板橋区常盤台4-32-9 泉ビル3F　　TEL.03-936-7706　FAX.03-936-7754

㈱アクス
インテリア・デザイン
AXE COMPANY LIMITED
Interior Design
AD, D:Hiroshi Takahara

GORO
Goro : Hair & Make up Studio

杉本こずえ

表参道店　〒107 東京都港区南青山5-3-25 Tel.03-498-5600

GORO
ヘア・メイクアップ
GORO
Hair/Make-up
AD, D:Masaaki Hiromura
D:Toshiyuki Kojima
DF:Studio Ikks.

KINEMA MOON
DISTINCTION DESIGN

Designer

木谷祥子
Sachiko Kitani

大阪市西区北堀江1-6-20 アバニテ四ッ橋701 Telephone 06-532-7280, Facsimile 06-532-7285

KINEMA MOON
デザイン
KINEMA MOON
Design
D:Yuichi Nakagawa

グラススタジオ クローブ
グラス・アーティスト
GLLASS STUDIO CLOVE
Glass Artist
AD, D, P: Satoshi Urimoto

イ・ピゼッリ
レストラン/バー
I PISELLI
Restaurant/Bar
D: Bigi Co., Ltd.

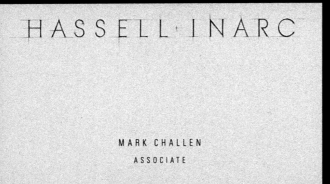

建築設計/インテリア・デザイン
HASSELL INARC
Architecture/Interior Design
DF: Emery Vincent Associates

有イクスース・アゴラ
グラフィックデザイン/企画
IKUSŪSU・AGORA CO., LTD.
Graphic Design/Planning
AD: Rutsu Tomita
D: Miyoko Kojima

日暮真三
SHINZO HIGURASHI
東京都中央区銀座4-14-15
サントル銀座401号 〒104
TELEPHONE 03（545）6124
FAXNUMBER 03（543）8254

日暮真三
コピーライター
SHINZO HIGURASHI
Copywriter
D:Keisuke Nagatomo
I:Seitaro Kuroda

写真家
栗岡 昌司

Office 古屋写真事務所 106 港区 西麻布 1-15-15 ドルメン西麻布 304 ☎03-479-3403

栗岡昌司
写真
MASASHI KURIOKA
Photography
AD, D:Nakaba Kozu

中 ■ 條 ■ 智 ■ 子

■157 東京都世田谷区南烏山 3-12-18-2 TEL 03（309）7693

中条智子
デザイン
TOMOKO CHUJO
Design
D:Tomoko Chujo

今 井 雅 巳
illustrator

㈲エボナイト・スタジオ
イラストレーション
EBONAITO-STUDIO CO.,LTD.
Illustration
I:Masami Imai

OFFICE
LEO
total satisfaction

代表
黒瀬よしみ

〒542 大阪市中央区東心斎橋1丁目20-9吉川ビル3F phone.06-243-7866 fax.06-243-7660

オフィス レオ
企画
OFFICE LEO
Planning
D:Taiko Okubo
DF:Office Mare

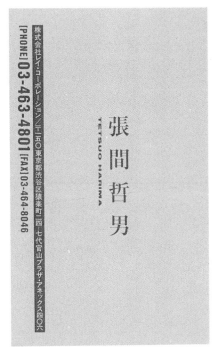

㈱レイコーポレーション
広告企画/制作
LEI CORPORATION
Advertising
AD, D:Minoru Niimi

㈱ディ アンド ディ スタジオ
設計/デザイン
D & D Studio Co., Ltd.
Planning/Design
AD:Rutsu Tomita
D:Miyoko Kojima
DF:Ikusûsu・Agora Co., Ltd.

美房
グッドデザイン・サプライヤー
BIBOU
Design Goods Supplier
AD, D:Hiromichi Otani

㈱シチュエーション
インテリア・デザイン
SITUATION CO., LTD.
Interior Design
AD, D:Hideki Horii

㈱プロパティインフォメーション
不動産業
PROPERTY INFORMATION INC.
Real Estate Agent
AD, D:Hiroshi Morishima

スペース デザイン オフィス ワッツニュー
インテリア・デザイン
SPACE DESIGN OFFICE WHAT NEW
Interior Design
AD, D:Takazo Imai
DF:Graphical, Voice

㈱仲畑広告制作所
広告制作
NAKAHATA COMPANY, LTD.
Advertising
D:Takashi Nakahata

桐ヶ谷昌行
個人用
MASAYUKI KIRIGAYA
Personal Use
D:Masayuki Kirigaya

㈲エヌパー・エモーショナル・インダストリィ
映像の企画/制作
n% EMOTIONAL INDUSTRY, INC.
Film Production
AD:Kuniji Nakai
D:Masayuki Takahashi

㈲水谷事務所
デザイン
MIZUTANI OFFICE
Design
AD, D:Koji Mizutani

矢田　陽
グラフィックデザイン
YADA YOH
Graphic Design
D:Yada Yoh

建築設計
TOWA ARCHITECTURE & DESIGN
Architecture/Design
AD, D:Pamela Virgilio

阿部かずお
イラストレーション/デザイン
KAZUO ABE
Illustration / Design
D: Kazuo Abe

若泉さな絵
イラストレーション
SANAE WAKAIZUMI
Illustration
D: Hisashi Miyake
I: Sanae Wakaizumi

㈲ウォーターボーイズ
プロダクション
WATERBOYS LTD.
PRODUCTION
D, I: Hiroyuki Ota
P: Masayuki Hatakeyama

村井 茜
イラストレーション
AKANE MURAI
Illustration
D: Shoko Fujiyama

神田和則
イラストレーション
KAZUNORI KANDA
Illustration
I:Kazunori Kanda

㈱海藤オフィス
照明デザイン
KAITO OFFICE INC.
Lighting Design
AD, D:Masaaki Hiromura
D:Takafumi Kusagaya
DF:Studio Ikks.

中安制作室
グラフィックデザイン
NAKAYASU CREATIVE STUDIO
Graphic Design
D:Yuji Nakayasu

奥田耕造
イラストレーション
KOZO OKUDA
Illustration
D, I:Kozo Okuda

㈱イトミアンドカンパニー
広告企画/制作
ITOMI & COMPANY
Advertising
AD, D:Komei Tanii

大塚 勉
写真
TSUTOMU OTSUKA
Photography
D:Tsutomu Otsuka

Sachiko Nakamura

3-3-2-#9 Aobadai, Meguro-ku, Tokyo 153, Japan
Tel / Fax 03-780-4462

中村幸子
イラストレーション
SACHIKO NAKAMURA
Illustration
I: Sachiko Nakamura

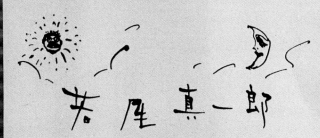

若尾真一郎

〒151 東京都渋谷区笹塚1-59-9-605　TEL. 03-377-4771

若尾真一郎
イラストレーション
SHINICHIRO WAKAO
Illustration
AD, D, I: Shinichiro Wakao

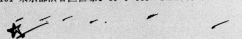

*Kuma

くまざわ の り こ

phone, fax　0774・31・8754

〒611　京都府宇治市五ヶ庄一番割53

くまざわのりこ
イラストレーション
NORIKO KUMAZAWA
Illustration
I: Noriko Kumazawa

荒 井 良 二

〒156 東京都世田谷区松原6-9-23
PHONE・03-323-3805

荒井良二
イラストレーション
RYOJI ARAI
Illustration
AD, D: Ryoji Arai

田代卓事務所
イラストレーション/グラフィックデザイン
TAKU TASHIRO OFFICE
Illustration/Graphic Design
I:Taku Tashiro

〒112 東京都文京区音羽1-17-11-605 Tel.03-946-3109

♪かわぐちせいこ

かわぐちせいこ
イラストレーション
SEIKO KAWAGUCHI
Illustration
D:Masashi Miyake

〒150 東京都渋谷区恵比寿1-11-12コーポ本多301号　TEL.(03)791-4625

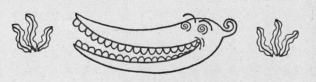

かわむらふゆみ
fuyumi kawamura

かわむらふゆみ
イラストレーション
FUYUMI KAWAMURA
Illustration
D, I:Fuyumi Kawamura

〒165　東京都中野区野方4-17-8　　TEL:03-385-2878

T O S H I O   N O M U R A

野村俊夫

野村俊夫
イラストレーション
TOSHIO NOMURA
Illustration
AD, D, I:Toshio Nomura

〒171　東京都豊島区南長崎5-21-2ハウススター南長崎301号
5-21-2-301, MINAMINAGASAKI, TOSHIMA-KU, TOKYO, 171, JAPAN
Tel./Fax. 03-953-4633

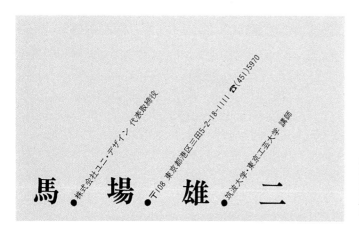

馬場雄二
グラフィックデザイン
YUJI BABA
Graphic Design
AD, D, :Yuji Baba
DF:Uni Design Co., Ltd.

佐
藤
宗
道

Photographer　Munemichi Sato

連絡先：株式会社クラッカースタジオ　Cracker Studio, Inc.

〒105 東京都港区虎ノ門5-3-13　芝中央マンション601号　電話03-433-5311〜3

#601 Shiba-chuo Mansion, 5-3-13 Toranomon, Minato-ku, Tokyo. Phone:03-433-5311〜3

佐藤宗道
写真
MUNEMICHI SATO
Photography
AD, D:Nobuo Abe
DF:Gong Inc.

川野隆司
イラストレーション
RYUJI KAWANO
Illustration
I:Ryuji Kawano

スコピオ・プロジェクト
パフォーマンス公演/制作
SCORPIO PROJECT
Performance Production
AD, D:Okinori Ohira

上原尚子
企画

東京都豊島区
東池袋 2 丁目
45-7 〒170
Tel. 03-988-1661
Fax.03-988-3391

サンヱオリジン株式会社

サンヱオリジン
婦人服飾製造販売
SAN e ORIGIN CO.,LTD.
Women's Fashion Manufacture/Sales
D:Hiromi Yanagisawa

Fashion Adviser
笠井 京子

LAUTRĒAMONT
vivre三宮 3F ロートレアモン ☎(078)391-6631(内・2467)

㈱ロートレ・アモン
アパレルメーカー/ショップ
LAUTRĒAMONT CO.,LTD.
Apparel Manufacture/Retail
AD, D, P, I:LautrēAmont Co.,Ltd.

集合 den
東京都文京区大塚4-51-1
電話番号 946-7567

稲葉宏爾
榊原加助
杉本幸夫
田中晃二
西俊章
保母恵
山口克巳
山本日出夫

集合 den
デザイン/編集
SHŪGŌ-den
Design/Editing
DF:Shūgō-den

代表取締役社長
古村 正幸
MASAYUKI KOMURA

inspec

インスペック コーポレーション
衣料品企画/デザイン/製造
INSPEC
Fashion Planning/Design/Manufacture
AD:Hiromichi Suzuki
D:Hiroshi Mozumi
DF:CR-Plot Co.,Ltd.

インスペック コーポレーション
〒156 東京都世田谷区松原1-28-7
TEL.03-323-4660. 323-4668 FAX.03-325-6741

青木美加子
フリーランサー
MIKAKO AOKI
Freelancer
D:Masashi Miyake

中村晃子
teruko nakamura   textile

東京都国分寺市新町 2-13-9

telephone＝
0423 (23) 3509

中村晃子
テキスタイル・デザイン
TERUKO NAKAMURA
Textile Design
AD, D:Sadao Sugaya

伊藤ともこ
スタイリスト
TOMOKO ITO
Stylist
D:AKIHIKO TSUKAMOTO

Face.
The Type Workshop.

Mike Chandler, Chairman, Face. The Type Workshop.
108A Miller Street, Pyrmont. (02) 552 3666, Fax (02) 552 1969.

タイプ・デザイン
FACE THE TYPE WORKSHOP
Type Design
DF:Face The Type Workshop

代表取締役
津 石 雅 実
MASAMI TSUISHI

株式会社 雅楽
〒545 大阪市阿倍野区阿倍野筋1-1-61新宿ビルB1
☎ 06-624-8643

㈱雅楽
レストラン/バー
GOURMET +BAR GARAKU
Restaurant/Bar
D:Seitaro Kuroda

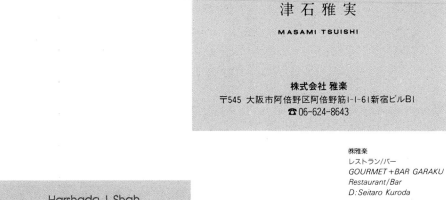

Harshada J. Shah

Orchids
ART OF EMBROIDERY
Contact.
Krishnabad, 4th floor,
43, Bhulabhai Desai Road, Bombay-400 026
☎ 822 1391

刺繍アート
ORCHIDS
Embroidery Art
AD, D:Sudarnshan Dheer

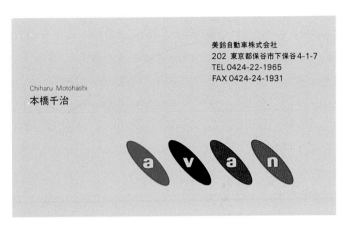

美鈴自動車株式会社
202 東京都保谷市下保谷4-1-7
TEL 0424-22-1965
FAX 0424-24-1931

Chiharu Motohashi
本橋千治

アバン（美鈴自動車㈱）
ヨーロッパの自動車代理店
AVAN (MISUZU MOTOR CO.,LTD.)
European Car Agency
AD, D:Hiromi Inayoshi

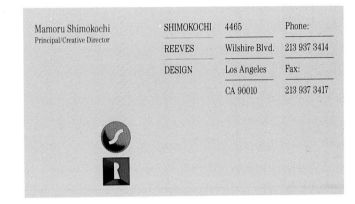

Mamoru Shimokochi
Principal/Creative Director

SHIMOKOCHI	4465	Phone:
REEVES	Wilshire Blvd.	213 937 3414
DESIGN	Los Angeles	Fax:
	CA 90010	213 937 3417

デザイン
SHIMOKOCHI/REEVES DESIGN
Design
AD, D:Mamoru shimokochi
AD:Anne Reeves
DF:Shimokochi/Reeves Design

KUNIJI NAKAI
President

▼n% EMOTIONAL INDUSTRY, Inc. Phone 03-478-0746
●THE 3rd VISUAL, Inc. Phone 03-478-3939
■A G'E-JAPAN Phone 03-478-0744
5F Kitamura Bldg. 4-10-6, Roppongi, Minato-ku,
Tokyo, Japan. Fax. No.03-478-0694
N.Y. OFFICE. Phone 914-347-2758, Fax 914-347-2759

㈲エヌパー・エモーショナル・インダストリィ
映像の企画/制作
n% EMOTIONAL INDUSTRY,INC.
Film Production
AD:Kuniji Nakai
D:Syoji Matsubara

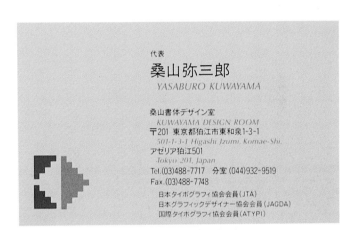

代表
桑山弥三郎
YASABURO KUWAYAMA

桑山書体デザイン室
KUWAYAMA DESIGN ROOM
〒201 東京都狛江市東和泉1-3-1
501-1-3-1 Higashi Izumi, Komae-Shi,
アゼリア狛江501
Tokyo 201, Japan
Tel.(03)488-7717　分室 (044)932-9519
Fax.(03)488-7748

日本タイポグラフィ協会会員（JTA）
日本グラフィックデザイナー協会会員（JAGDA）
国際タイポグラフィ協会会員（ATYPI）

桑山書体デザイン室
ロゴ・デザイン
KUWAYAMA DESIGN ROOM
Typeface Design
AD, D:Yasaburo Kuwayama

アート・ディレクター
赤羽なつみ

株式会社 ゾナルト アンド カンパニー
■本社 150 東京都渋谷区神山町9・5
PHONE.03·467·4471 FAX.03·467·4494
■大阪事務所 540 大阪市中央区内平野町2-3-1 503
PHONE.06-945-4737 FAX. 06-945-4482
■商品センター 418 静岡県富士宮市外神押出2188
PHONE.0544-58-5236 FAX. 0544-58-3789

㈱ゾナルト アンド カンパニー
ラッピンググッズの製造販売
ZONART & Co.,Ltd.
Wrapping Goods Manufacture/Retail
CD:Katsu Kimura
AD:Natsumi Akabane
D:Isao Sakamoto

株式会社日本デザインセンター
〒104 東京都中央区銀座1-13-13中央大和ビル
電話03-567-3231(代表)

総合グラフィックス研究室 デザインディレクター
中川憲造
Nakagawa kenzo

NDCグラフィックス
グラフィックデザイン
NDC GRAPHICS
Graphic Design
AD:Kenzo Nakagawa
D:Hiroyasu Nobuyama

SBK Records

SBK Records

SBK Records

Gary H. Klein
Vice President, Creative Services

1290 Avenue of the Americas
New York, New York 10104   (212) 492-1249
Telex 175604   Telefax (212) 245-4115

1290 Avenue of the Americas   New York, New York 10104

1290 Avenue of the Americas   New York, New York 10104   Telephone (212) 492-1200

Telex 175604   Telefax (212) 245-4115

レコード会社
SBK RECORDS
Record Company
AD, I:Nancy Skolos
D:Cheryl Lilley Shea
DF:Skolos Wedell Inc.

デザイン
GREENEVASEN/VANDER SCHANS
Design
AD, D:Robert van Rixtel

ミュージカル・グループ
QUANTUM
Musical Group
AD, D, I:Fernando Medina
DF:F. Medina Design

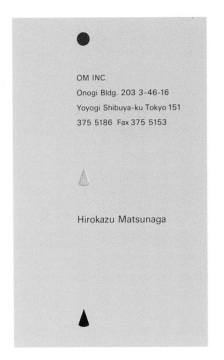

ポスター/プリント・ショップ
IMPRINTS
Poster/Print Shop
AD, D, I:Valerie Wong
DF:The Design Office of Wong & Yeo

㈱オム
建築設計/インテリア
OM INC.
Architecture/Interiors
AD, D:Hiromi Inayoshi

NAME   NO.

㈱ロートレ・アモン
アパレルメーカー/ショップ
LAUTRĒAMONT CO.,LTD.
Apparel Manufacture/Retail
AD, D, P, I:Lautrēamont Co.,Ltd.

カメラ・サービス
SHOOTING GALLERY
Camera Services
AD:Rick Eiber
D:J.Wason
DF:Rick Eiber Design

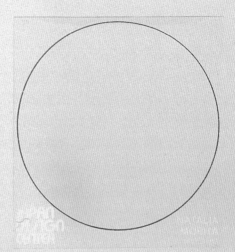

デザイン
JAPAN DESIGN CENTER
Design
D:Minoru Morita

アーバンデザイン企画室
高石昌文
徳島市金沢2丁目1番10-305   TEL・FAX(0886)64-3460
鳴門市撫養町大桑島北ノ浜81-301   TEL・FAX(0886)86-0485

アーバンデザイン
ショップ・デザイン
A~VAN DESIGN
Store Design
AD:Masafumi Takaishi
D:Hatsumi Takaishi

Law rence

Box 224
Ojai CA 93023

Lan off

CA   805.646.4549
NY   212.675.6224

映画監督
LAW RENCE LAN OFF
Film Direction
AD, D:Pamela Virgilio

HEAD + HEART
GRAPHIC ART VISUAL DESIGN~ATELIER

渡部隆志
TAKASHI WATANABE

ヘッド プラス ハート
デザイン
HEAD+HEART
Design
D:Takashi Watanabe

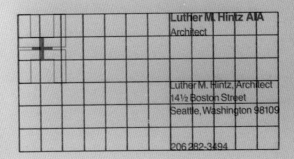

Luther M. Hintz AIA
Architect

Luther M. Hintz, Architect
14½ Boston Street
Seattle, Washington 98109

206 282-3494

建築設計
LUTHER M. HINTZ AIA
Architecture
AD, D:Rick Eiber
DF:Rick Eiber Design

広告宣伝/企画
BIG TIME PRODUCTIONS
Public Relations/Marketing/Promotion
AD, D, I:James W. Keaton
DF:GK+D Communications Inc.

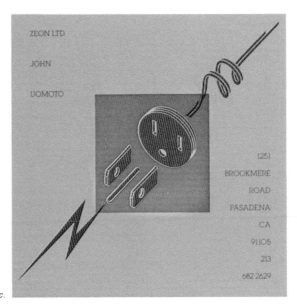

062 RO1-12
ビジネス・コンサルタント
ZEON LTD
Business Consulting
AD, D, I:Bill Tom
DF:Rod Dyer Group, Inc.

グラフィックデザイン
MCLEAN DESIGN
Graphic Design
AD, D, I:Eric Jon Read

加藤禎生
会社員
YORIO KATO
Office Worker
AD, D:Yorio Kato

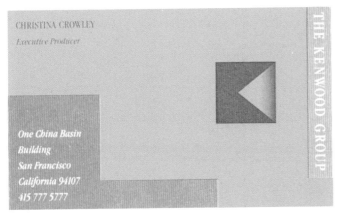

映画/ビデオ制作
THE KENWOOD GROUP
Film/Video Post Production
AD, D, I:Hock Wah Yeo
I:Chris Kirby
DF:The Design Office of Wong & Yeo

グラフィックデザイン
ROSS CARRON DESIGN
Graphic Design
AD, D:Ross Carron
DF:Carron Design

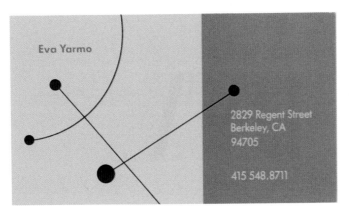

個人用
EVA YARMO
Personal Use
AD, D:Ross Carron
DF:Carron Design

建築設計
FEEMUNSON EBERT
Architecture
AD, D:Ross Carron
DF:Carron Design

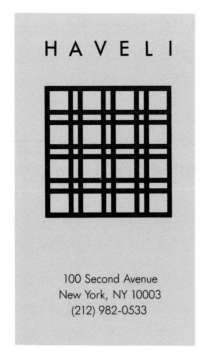

HAVELI

100 Second Avenue
New York, NY 10003
(212) 982-0533

レストラン
HAVELI
Restaurant
D:Vishva Peea

HARRY METZLER ARTDESIGN

BRAND 774
A-6867 SCHWARZENBERG
AUSTRIA/EUROPE
TELEPHONE 0 55 12 34 94
TELEFAX 0 55 12 34 94

グラフィックデザイン
HARRY METZLER DE・LUXE ART DESIGN
Graphic Design
AD, D:Harry Metzler
DF:Harry Metzler Artdesign

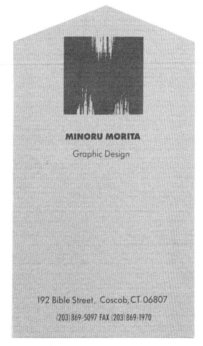

MINORU MORITA

Graphic Design

192 Bible Street, Coscob, CT. 06807
(203) 869-5097 FAX (203) 869-1970

グラフィックデザイン
MINORU MORITA
Graphic Design
D:Minoru Morita

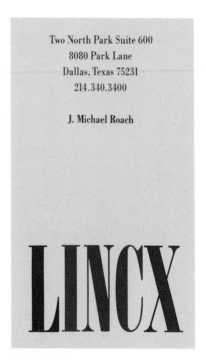

Two North Park Suite 600
8080 Park Lane
Dallas, Texas 75231
214.340.3400

J. Michael Roach

LINCX

経営コンサルタント
LINCX INC.
Financial Consultants
AD:Michael Stanard
D:Marcos Chavez
DF:Michael Stanard Inc.

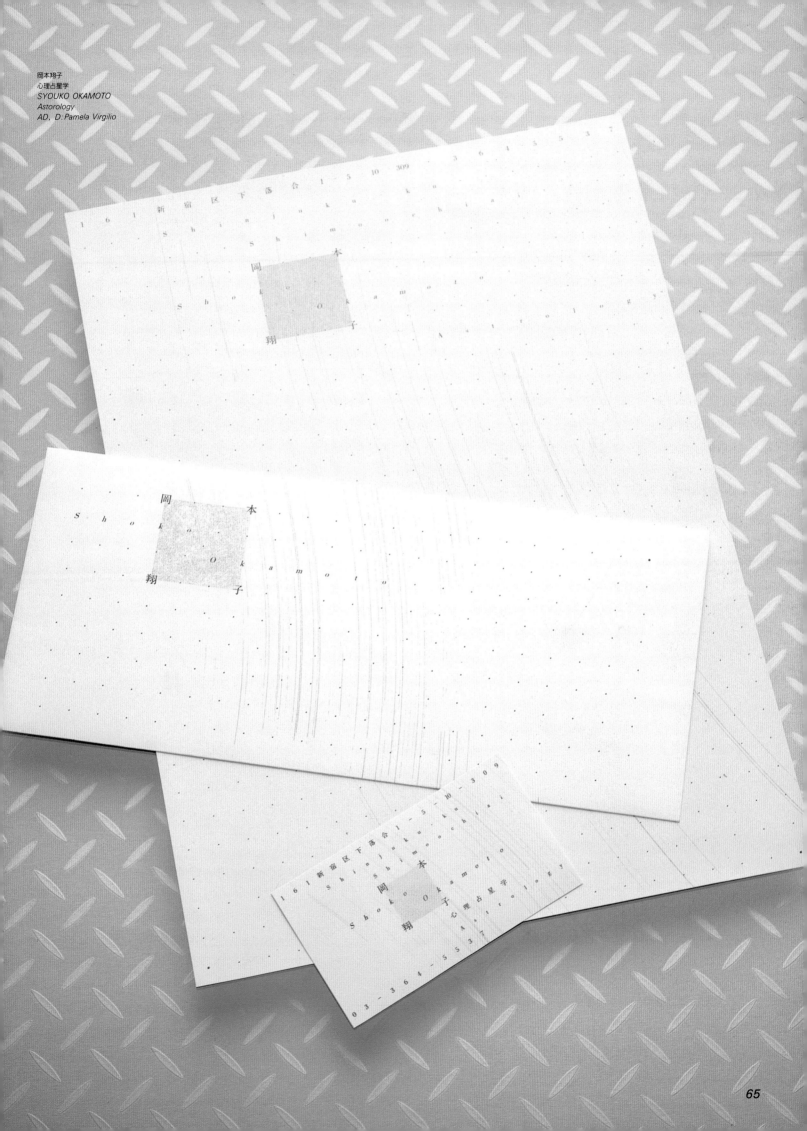

岡本翔子
心理占星学
SYOUKO OKAMOTO
Astorology
AD, D:Pamela Virgilio

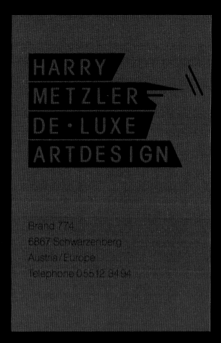

クラフィックテサイン
HARRY METZLER DE・LUXE ART DESIGN
Graphic Design
AD, D:Harry Metzler
DF:Harry Metzler Artdesign

Brand 774
6867 Schwarzenberg
Austria/Europe
Telephone 05512 3494

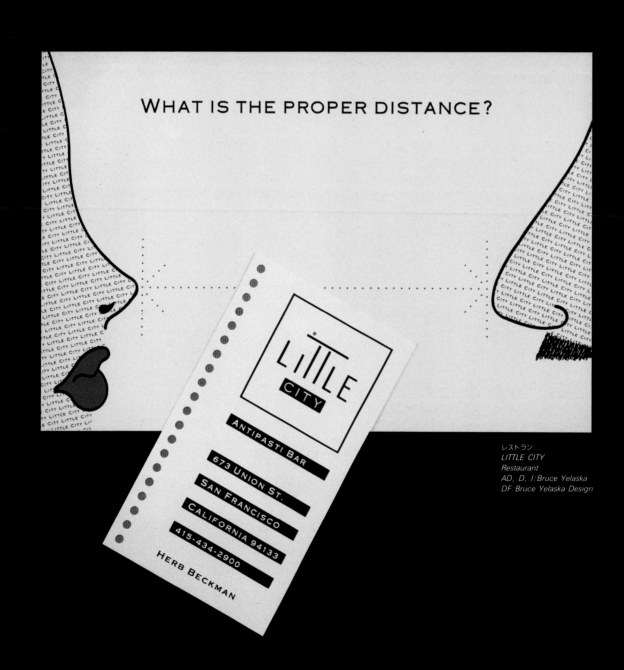

WHAT IS THE PROPER DISTANCE?

レストラン
LITTLE CITY
Restaurant
AD, D, I:Bruce Yelaska
DF:Bruce Yelaska Design

The Body & Bath Shop

Oggo
Doug Arnett
221 Tenth Avenue S.W.
Calgary Alberta Canada T2R 0A4
Telephone. 403 237 6446 Fax. 403 237 7629

Gregory Gregory Limited
Ian Gregory
Design Consultant
1081 River Road
Ottawa Canada K1K 3V9
(613) 741-4027

ボディ アンド バス ショップ
ショップ
THE BODY AND BATH SHOP
Shop
AD Ryoichi Kojima
D Takeshi Abe

オッゴ デザイン ショップ
OGGO DESIGN SHOP ltd.
Design Shop
Oggo Design Shop Ltd.

デザイン
GREGORY GREGORY LIMITED
Design
AD Judith Gregory
D Ian Gregory
DF Gregory Gregory Limited

67

ワイン会社
SHADOW CREEK CELLARS
Winery
AD, D, I:Hock Wah Yeo
I:Carry Chiao
DF:The Design Office of Wong & Yeo

繊維商社
TAKIHYO INC.
Textile Firm

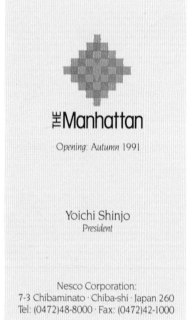

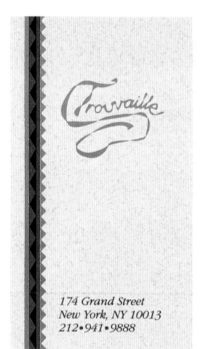

ホテル開発
NESCO CORPORATION
Hotel Development
DF:UCI Inc.

レストラン
YROUVAILLE
Restaurant
D:Paradeign Design

ジュエリー・サロン
FACERE
Jewelry Salon
AD, D:Jack Anderson
D:Cliff Chung
I:Bruce Hale
DF:Hornall Anderson Design Works

不動産業
EUROIMMOBILIARE
Real Estate Agent
AD, D:Fabio Adranno

JAMES E. DELANY
COMMISSIONER

1111 PLAZA DRIVE
SCHAUMBURG, ILLINOIS
60173-4990

708/605-8933

THE BIG TEN CONFERENCE

大学協議会
BIG TEN CONFERENCE
Collegiate Events
AD:Michael Stanard
D:Lisa Finger Hut
DF:Michael Stanard Inc.

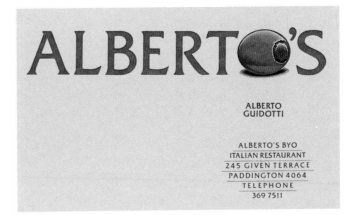

ALBERTO'S

ALBERTO
GUIDOTTI

ALBERTO'S BYO
ITALIAN RESTAURANT
245 GIVEN TERRACE
PADDINGTON 4064
TELEPHONE
369 7511

イタリアン・レストラン
ALBERTO'S
Italian Restaurant
AD, D:Dennis Veal
I:John Morris

Eye Care Clinic & Surgi-Center

Worldster Lee, M.D.

Liliha Medical Building
1712 Liliha Street • Suite 400 • Honolulu • Hawaii 96817

Telephone: (808) 524-1010

眼科診療所
EYE CARE CLINIC & SURGI-CENTER
Eye Care Clinic
DF:UCI Inc.

CONSTRUCTIVE SOLUTIONS

1740 Ridge Avenue

Jeanne Breslin

Evanston, Illinois 60201

708.864.9360

コンピューター建築
CONSTRUCTIVE SOLUTIONS
Computer Architecture
AD:Michael Stanard
D, I:Marcos Chavez
DF:Michael Stanard Inc.

Suzanne Weiss
Director of Marketing
& Sales

Sawtooth Software

1007 Church Street
Suite 302
Evanston, Illinois
60201
312/866-0870

コンピューター・ソフトウェア
SAWTOOTH SOFTWARE
Computer Software
AD:Michael Stanard
D, I:Ann Werner
DF:Michael Stanard Inc.

Cellular
One

Lawrence R. Childs
Executive Vice President

P.O. Box 9159
Seattle, WA 98109-0159
201 Elliott Avenue West, Suite 220
Seattle, WA 98119-4216
206·284·5555 Mobile 972·1080

CELLULAR
AD, D:Jack Anderson
D:Raymond Terada
I:NA
DF:Hornall Anderson Design Works

歯科医
KENT R.BROWN,D.D.S.
Dentist
AD, D, I: Robert Walter
DF: Robert Walter Advertising

歯科医
JOHN R.SECHENA
Dentist
AD, D: Jack Anderson
I: NA
DF: Hornall Anderson Design Works

Kent R. Brown, D.D.S.
Family Dentistry
4805 River Oaks Blvd.
Fort Worth, Texas 76114
(817) 625-1548

General Dentistry
for Adults &
Children

John R.
Sechena
D.D.S.

11749
Greenwood
Ave. N.

Seattle,
Washington
98133

Phone:
Off. 363-8777
Res. 783-4325

Office
Hours by
Appointment

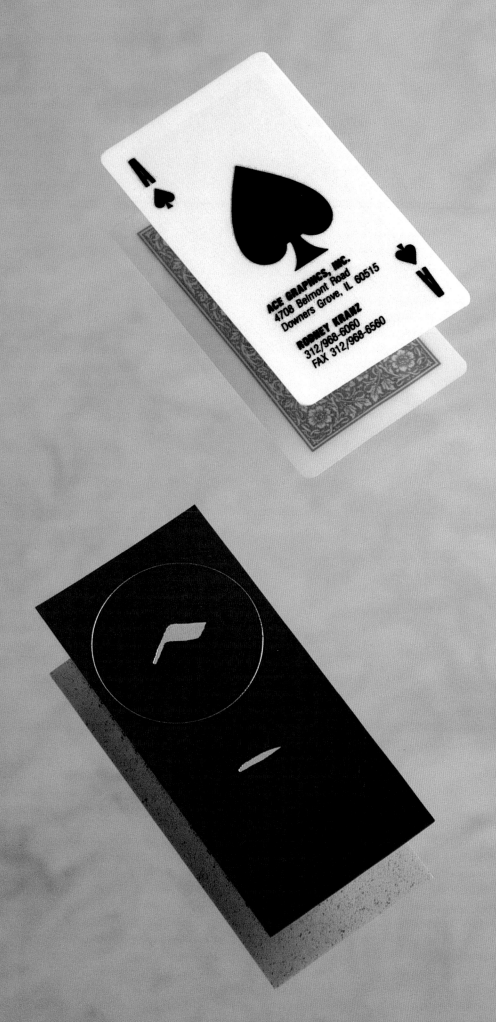

ACE GRAPHICS, INC.
4708 Belmont Road
Downers Grove, IL 60515

RODNEY KRANZ
312/968-6060
FAX 312/968-6560

グラフィックデザイン
ACE GRAPHILS
Graphic Design
AD:Michael Stanard
D:Lyle Zimmerman
DF:Michael Stanard Inc.

展示会装飾レンタル
NOEL LOCATION
Public Event Tent/Accessories Rental
AD, D, I:Catherine Zask

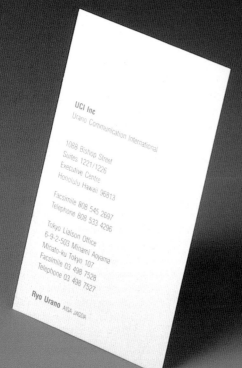

UCI Inc
Urano Communication International

1088 Bishop Street
Suites 1221/1226
Executive Centre
Honolulu Hawaii 96813

Facsimile 808 545 2697
Telephone 808 533 4296

Tokyo Liaison Office
6-9-2-503 Minami Aoyama
Minato-ku Tokyo 107
Facsimile 03 498 7528
Telephone 03 498 7527

Ryo Urano AIGA JAGDA

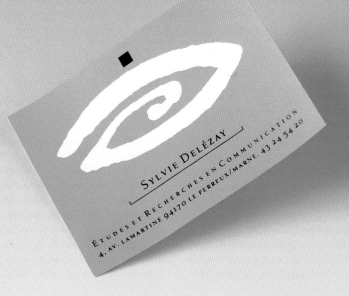

SYLVIE DELÉZAY

ÉTUDES ET RECHERCHES EN COMMUNICATION

4, AV. LAMARTINE 94170 LE PERREUX/MARNE. 43 24 54 20

デザイン/企画
UCI INC.
Design/Communication
DF:UCI Inc.

証券会社
R.T.JONE
Capital Equities
AD, D, I:David Chiow

コミュニケーション・アドバイザー
DELEZAY COMMUNICATION
Communication Adviser
AD, D, I:Catherine Zask

麹谷・入江デザイン室
グラフィックデザイン/企画制作
KOJITANI, IRIE & INC
Graphic Design/Planning
AD：Hiroshi Kojitani
D：Kensuke Irie

㈱シーズコンサルティンググループ
経営コンサルティング
SEEDS CONSULTING GROUP CO.,LTD.
Management Consulting
AD, D：Toshihiro Onimaru
D：Keisuke Yoshikawa

ダイアナ デリックス デザインズ
デザイン
DIANA DERICKS DESIGNS
Design
AD, D:Ryo Urano
A:Tracy Asari

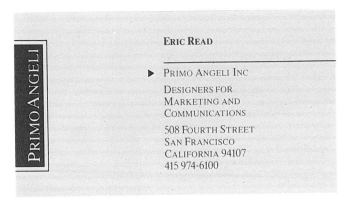

ERIC READ

► PRIMO ANGELI INC

DESIGNERS FOR
MARKETING AND
COMMUNICATIONS

508 FOURTH STREET
SAN FRANCISCO
CALIFORNIA 94107
415 974-6100

グラフィックデザイン
PRIMO ANGELI
Graphic Design
AD, D, I:Eric Jon Read

TINA R. CORSON

SWEEPING CHANGES, INC.
990 WEST FULLERTON, SUITE 180
CHICAGO, ILLINOIS 60614

312-975-6691

ほうき会社
SWEEPING CHANGES, INC.
Broom Company
AD:Michael Stanard
D, I:Ann Werner
DF:Michael Stanard Inc.

LES M WONG D.D.S.

827 Blossom Hill Rd.

Suite W-3

San Jose

California 95123

408 224.2000

歯科医
LESM WONG DDS
Dentist
AD, D, I:Valerie Wong
DF:The Design Office of Wong & Yeo

DAVID FRENCH / SIGN PAINTER
1249 16th Ave #5 / San Francisco / Ca / 94122 / 415 664-8394

看板屋
DAVID FRENCH
Sign Painting
AD, D, I:Valerie Wong
DF:The Design Office of Wong & Yeo

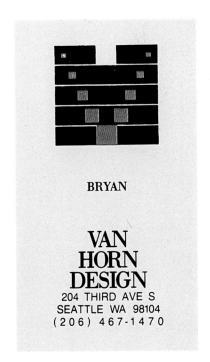

BRYAN

VAN
HORN
DESIGN
204 THIRD AVE S
SEATTLE WA 98104
(206) 467-1470

注文家具
VAN HORN DESIGN
Custom Commercial Furniture
AD, D, I:Cliff Chung
DF:Hornall Anderson Design Works

写真
DAVID VAN DIJK
Photography
AD, D:Shigeru Watano

新日本製鉄㈱
製鉄会社
NIPPON STEEL CORPORATION
Iron Industry
CD:Toshifumi Kawahara
AD:Kenzo Nakagawa
D:Satoshi Morikami
DF:NDC Graphics

Carlos Navajas
Fotógrafo
Vinaroz 16-B-3-11
28002 Madrid Spain
Tel. 415 50 35

写真
CARLOS NAVAJAS
Photography
AD, D, I:Fernando Medina
DF:F. Medina Design

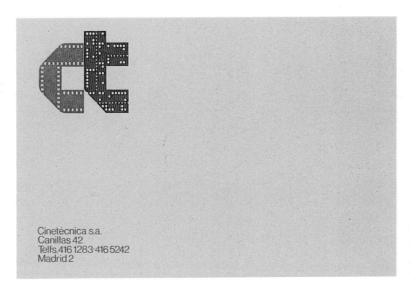

Cinetécnica s.a.
Canillas 42
Telfs.416 1283·416 5242
Madrid 2

映画プロデューサー
CINE TECNICA
Film Production
AD, D, I:Fernando Medina
DF:F. Medina Design

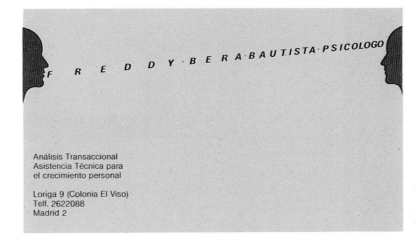

FREDDY·BERA·BAUTISTA·PSICOLOGO

Análisis Transaccional
Asistencia Técnica para
el crecimiento personal

Loriga 9 (Colonia El Viso)
Telf. 2622088
Madrid 2

心理学者
FREDDY BERA
Psychology
AD, D, I:Fernando Medina
DF:F. Medina Design

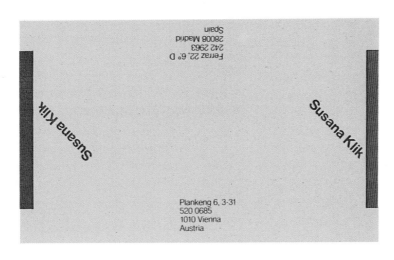

Susana Klik

Ferraz 22, 6° D
242 2963
28008 Madrid
Spain

Plankeng 6, 3-31
520 0685
1010 Vienna
Austria

デザイン
SUSANA KLIK
Design
AD, D, I:Fernando Medina
DF:F. Medina Design

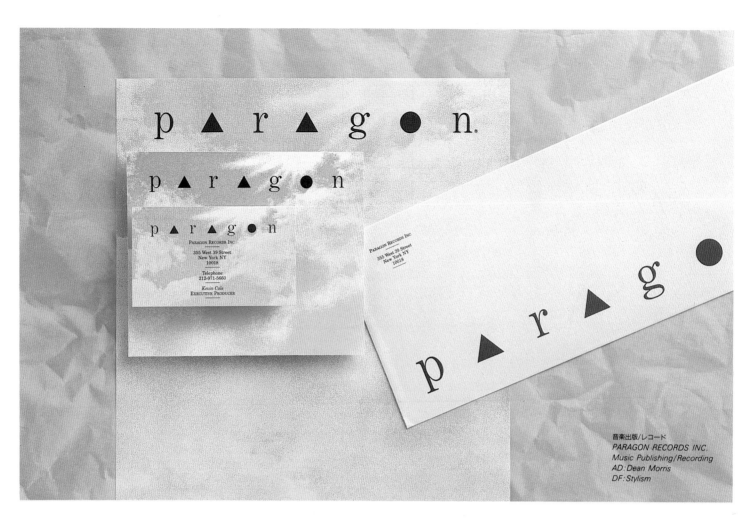

音楽出版/レコード
PARAGON RECORDS INC.
Music Publishing/Recording
AD:Dean Morris
DF:Stylism

グラフィックデザイン
THE DESIGN OFFICE OF WONG & YEO
Graphic Design
AD, D, I:Hock Wah Yeo
DF:The Design Office of Wong & Yeo

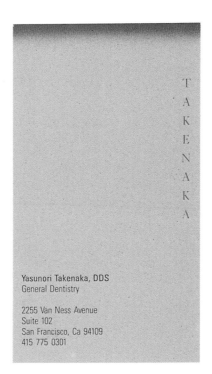

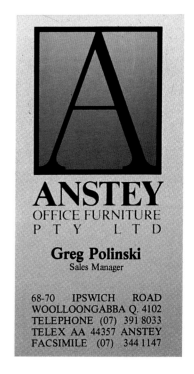

ショップ
HOSHONI-ELLEN KNIGHT
Retail
AD, D:Anna Demchick

歯科医
TAKENAKA DDS
Dentist
AD, D, I:Valerie Wong
DF:The Design Office of Wong & Yeo

家具メーカー
ANSTEY OFFICE FURNITURE
Furniture Manufacture
AD, D, I:Dennis Veal

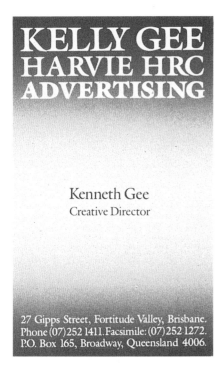

広告代理店
KELLY GEE HARVIE HRC
Advertising Agency
AD, D:Dennis Veal
I:John Morris

本屋
PETER MILLER BOOKS
Book Store
AD, D, I:Tim Girvin Design, Inc.
DF:Tim Girvin Design, Inc.

歯科医
LEE DDS/HIROSE DDS/WONG DDS
Dentist
AD, D, I:Valerie Wong
I:Chris Kirby
DF:The Design Office of Wong & Yeo

The DESK of TAKAYUKI MITSUNAGA
302. 17-7 Nanpeidai-cho,
Shibuya-ku, Tokyo 150, Japan
Phone 03-463-2962
TAKAYUKI MITSUNAGA

Produktieleiding
Film-Video

H

N   S

-Groenwold

Czaar Peterstraat 126²
1018.PV Amsterdam
Telefoon 020-24 44 12

MONDO CANE

CUCINA REGIONALE

(212) 254-5166

205 THOMPSON ST., NYC

S   W

W

N

Rod Dyer
Group, Inc.

Design &
Advertising

8360 Melrose Ave.

3rd Floor

Los Angeles

CA 90069

213 655-1800

FAX 213 655-9159

S

小永尚之
コピーライター
TAKAYUKI MITSUNAGA
Copywriter
AD: D Yoshiro Kajitani
P Chojiro Nitta
CW. Takayuki Mitsungga

映画制作
HANS GROENWOLD
Film-Production
AD: D. Frans Lieshout

ショップ
MONDO CANE
Retail

広告/デザイン
ROD DYER GROUP, INC
Design/Advertising
AD: D Steve Twigger
I Phil Leith
DF Rod Dyer Group, Inc

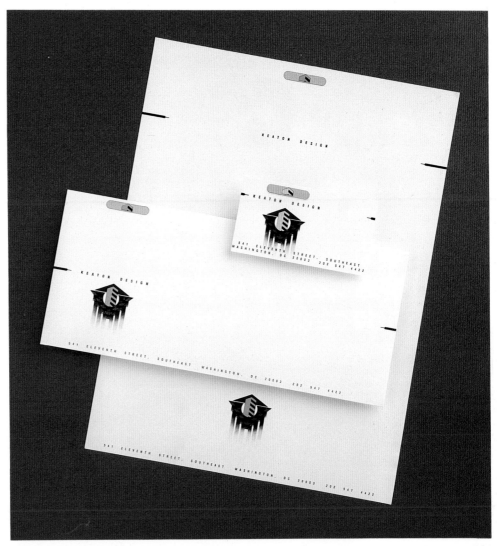

グラフィックデザイン
KEATON DESIGN
Graphic Design
AD, D, I:James W. Keaton

デリカテッセン・チェーン
ULTRA LUCCA DELICATESSEN, INC.
Delicatessen Chain
AD, D:Primo Angeli
I:Mark Jones
DF:Primo Angeli Inc.

ラジオ・ステーション
KNHC 89 GM
Radio Station
AD, D:John Hornall
D:Juliet Shen/Julie Tanagi-Lock
I:NA
DF:Hornall Anderson Design Works

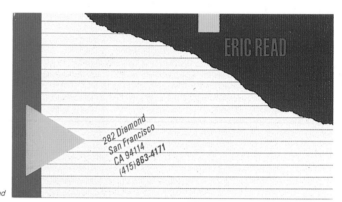

グラフィックデザイン
ERIC JON READ
Graphic Design
AD, D, I:Eric Jon Read

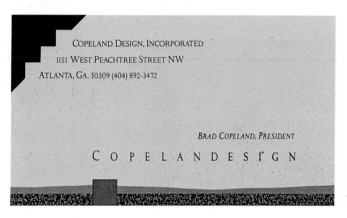

デザイン
COPELAND DESIGN INC.
Design
AD, D:Brad Copeland
DF:Copeland Design Inc.

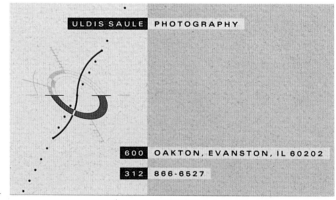

写真
ULDIS SAULE
Photography
AD:Michael Stanard
D, I:Lyle Zimmerman
DF:Michael Stanard Inc.

CAMBRIDGE FURNITURE COLLECTIONS

438 Massachusetts Avenue   Cambridge MA 02139 USA

CAMBRIDGE FURNITURE COLL

617.
864.
3300

TEL
4973990 C

438 Massachusetts Avenue   Cambridge MA 02139 USA

Wendy Glomb
Director

438 Massachusetts Avenue
Cambridge, Massachusetts 02139

617 864 3300

Telex 4973990 CMBFURN

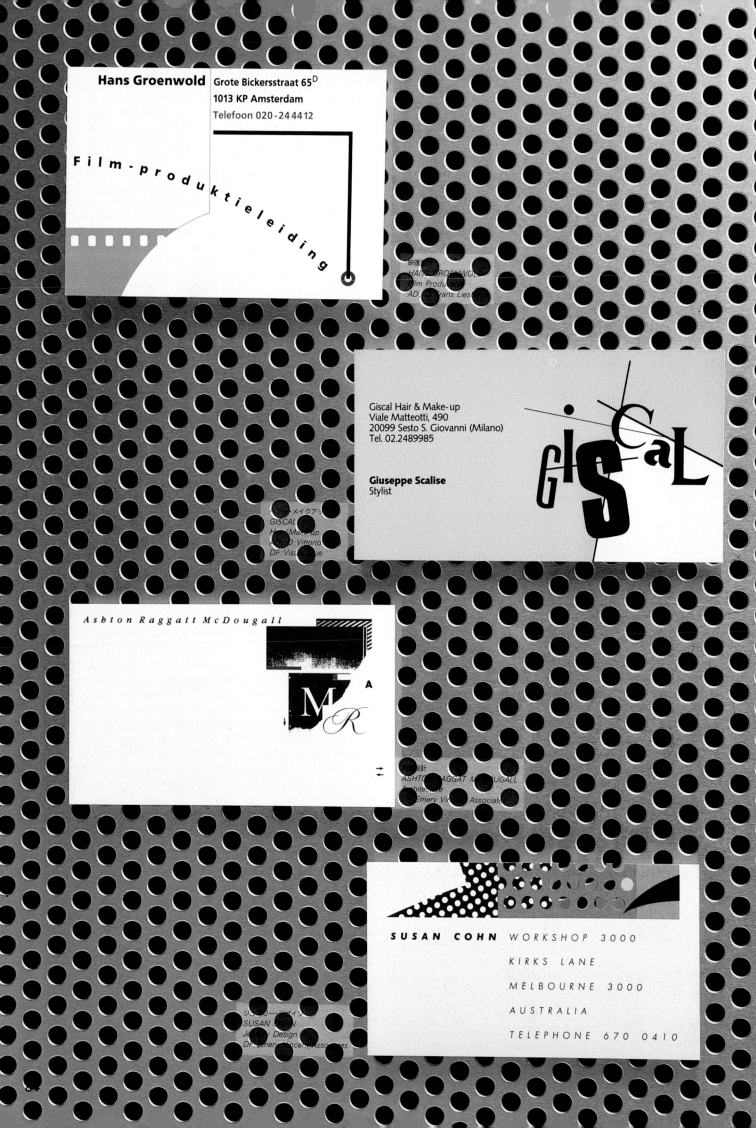

Hans Groenwold Grote Bickersstraat 65ᴰ
1013 KP Amsterdam
Telefoon 020-244412

F i l m - p r o d u k t i e l e i d i n g

映画制作
HANS GROENWOLD
Film Production
AD, D: Frans Lieshout

Giscal Hair & Make-up
Viale Matteotti, 490
20099 Sesto S. Giovanni (Milano)
Tel. 02.2489985

Giuseppe Scalise
Stylist

GiScaL

ヘア/メイクアップ
GISCAL
Hair/Make-up
AD, D: Vittorio...
DF: Visual...que

Ashton Raggatt McDougall

設計
ASHTON RAGGAT McDOUGALL
Architecture
DF: Emery Vincent Associates

SUSAN COHN WORKSHOP 3000

KIRKS LANE

MELBOURNE 3000

AUSTRALIA

TELEPHONE 670 0410

ジュエリー・デザイン
SUSAN COHN
Jewelry Design
DF: Emery Vincent Associates

写真
BEN KERNS
Photography
AD, D:Rick Eiber
DF:Rick Eiber Design

写真
ROBERT VAN RIXTEL
Photography
AD, D:Robert van Rixtel
DF:Total Design

エフ エム ジャパン
ラジオ放送局
FM·JAPAN
Radio Station
AD, D:Masahisa Nakamura

デザイン
F. MEDINA DESIGN
Design
AD, D, I:Fernando Medina
DF:F. Medina Design

FARM DIGITAL RECORDING STUDI O

DIEGO SANDRIN
executive producer

Tel. 0421/53755-53233
Fax 0421/53775-53233
Via Calnotta Vecchia, 21/A
31016 Cessalto (Tv) Italy

MARWOOD

Ross Wood

MARWOOD COMMERCIAL FURNITURE
(Lampson Pty. Ltd. as trustee for the Lampson Discretionary Trust)
MANUFACTURERS AND SUPPLIERS OF QUALITY CUSTOM-BUILT FURNITURE
31 GODWIN STREET PO BOX 143 BULIMBA QUEENSLAND 4171 PHONE (07) 399 1533

EINBAUSCHRÄNKE FÜR TÜREN UND FACHBETRIEB ● PISCHKE INNENAUSBAUTEN ● INDIVIDUELLE MÖBEL ● TEL. 07031/27 23 58 ● WANDVERKLEIDUNG ● STR. 18 7030 BÖBLINGEN

Riki
Yamanaka Constractions

レコーディングスタジオ
FARM DIGITAL RECORDING STUDIO
Recording Studio
AD, D: Hermano Corti

家具メーカー
MAR WOOD
Furniture Manufacture
AD, D: Dennis Veal
John Morris

家具師
BENIRS CHKE
Cabinet Maker
AD, D: Hands George Lang

山中建設
YAMANAKA CONSTRACTIONS
Contractors
AD, D: Tatsuki Yasuda

William E. Carter
Builder/Developer

P.O. Box 661865
Sacramento
California 95866
1·916·489·4147

Pager
1·916·328·8985

FAX
1·916·482·7306

William E. Carter
Builder/Developer

P.O. Box 661865
Sacramento
California 95866
1·916·489·4147

Pager
1·916·328·8985

FAX
1·916·482·7306

William E. Carter
Builder/Developer

P.O. Box 661865
Sacramento
California 95866

建設業/デベロッパー
WILLIAM E. CARTER
Construction/Development
AD, D: Michael Kennedy
DF: Michael Kennedy Associates

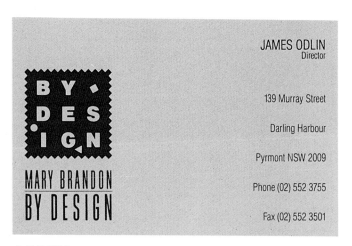

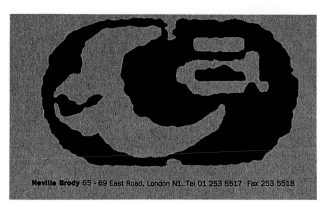

JAMES ODLIN
Director

139 Murray Street

Darling Harbour

Pyrmont NSW 2009

Phone (02) 552 3755

Fax (02) 552 3501

インテリア・デザイン
MARY BRANDON-BY DESIGN
Interior Design
AD, D:Mamoru shimokochi
AD:Anne Reeves
DF:Shimokochi/Reeves Design

デザイン
NEVILLE BRODY
Design
AD, D, I:Neville Brody

アート/ミュージック・エージェント
CCC
Art/Music Representation
AD, D, I:Neville Brody

ヤマダノブオ
イラストレーション
NOBUO YAMADA
Illustration
I:Nobuo Yamada

1303 J Street
Suite 517
Sacramento, CA 95814
916/443-7817

Gale R. Kaufman

OFFICIAL BALLOT

政治関係
KAUFMAN CAMPAIGN CONSULTANTS
Political
AD, D:Michael Kennedy

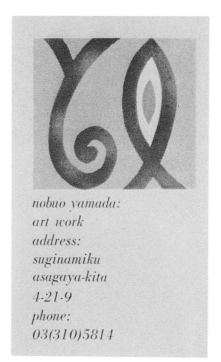

nobuo yamada:
art work
address:
suginamiku
asagaya-kita
4-21-9
phone:
03(310)5814

ヤマダノブオ
イラストレーション
NOBUO YAMADA
Illustration
I:Nobuo Yamada

㈱ジャパングラフィックス
広告企画/制作
JAPAN GRAPHICS CORPORATION
Advertising
D:Yasuyuki Ito

㈱メンズ・ビギ
アパレルメーカー
MEN'S BIGI CO.,LTD.
Apparel Maker
AD; D:Neville Brody

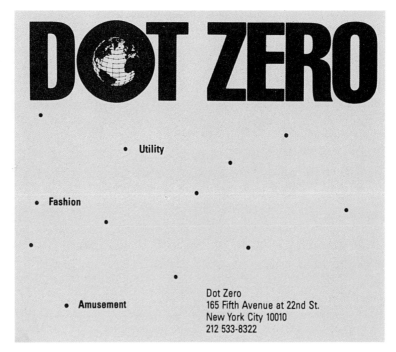

Dot Zero
165 Fifth Avenue at 22nd St.
New York City 10010
212 533-8322

デザイン
DOT ZERO
Design Shop
D: Gail Rigelmaupt

クラブ マルヤマ
ディスコ/レストラン/バー
CLUB MARUYAMA
Discotheque/Restaurant/Bar
AD, D: Hiroshi Takahara

スポーツ・ストアー
CLARK'S
Sports Store
D: Greenberg Displays

JUAN JOSE AROZTEGUI · ARQUITECTURA

Bendición de Campos 10 Teléfono 2509555 Madrid 16

建築設計
JJA
Architecture
AD, D, I: Fernando Medina
DF: F. Medina Design

加藤倫子
主婦
MICHIKO KATO
Homemaker
AD, D:Yorio Kato

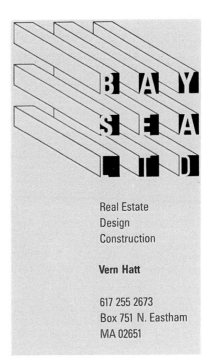

建設会社
BAY SEA LTD.
Construction
AD, D:Pamela Virgilio

レストラン
SHELBY
Restaurant

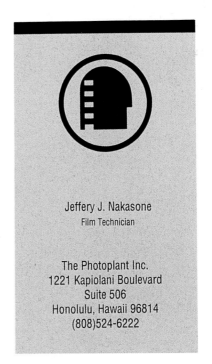

THE PHOTOPLANT INC.
AD, D:Roger Yu
DF:Goodson+Yu Design

栗 原 勝
代表取締役 社長

浜松都市開発株式会社
〒430 静岡県浜松市板屋町111-2
Tel (0534)-53-7900
Fax(0534)-53-7901

S H I R A S A G I
japanese restaurant

A.L. Abbink
direkteur

Spui 170 2511 BW Den Haag telefoon 070 - 46 47 00

I

B O T A N I C A L

㈱フォルテ
都市開発
FORTE CO., LTD
City Development
AD Tetsuya Harada
D Fumio Ogawa

日本料理店
SHIRASAGI
Japanese Restaurant
AD・D Shigeru Watano

レストラン/ホテル
BOTANICAL HOTEL
Restaurant/Hotel
DF Emery Vincent Associates

渡辺 明

株式会社 渡辺 明 設計事務所
〒152 東京都目黒区碑文谷2-20-26
電話03-710-1963 Fax.03-710-1872

渡辺明設計事務所
建築設計
AKIRA WATANABE ARCHITECTS ASSOCIATES
Architecture
AD:Ryohei Kojima
D:Takeshi Abe

代表取締役

中 山 浩 一

有限会社 ムッシュ倶楽部
山口県宇部市小串中堀401
Tel.0836(35)0500 Fax.0836(35)0501

㈲ムッシュ倶楽部
輸入雑貨小売
MONSIEUR CLUB CO., LTD.
Import Goods Retail
DF:Sugar Pot

VANDERBEEK & CHIOW

130 S. BEMISTON AVE.
SUITE 708
ST. LOUIS, MO. 63105
314.721.1767

ADVERTISING
PROMOTION
DESIGN

DAVID CHIOW

広告/デザイン
VANDER BEEK & CHIOW
Advertising/Design
AD, D, I:David Chiow

YAMA   GUCHI
AKIRA

山 口 朗 〒185東京都国分寺市光町2-9-30-B PHONE／FAX0425(77)2558

山口 朗
グラフィックデザイン/イラストレーション
AKIRA YAMAGUCHI
Graphic Design/Illustration
AD:Akira Yamaguchi

"soap"
THE GRAPHIC LAUNDRY INC.

03-400-3513
FAX·406-6697
4F HOKKOKU BUILDING, 3·2·1 SHIBUYA,
SHIBUYA·KU, TOKYO 150 JAPAN

代表取締役 *Isao Sakai Creative Director*
酒井　治　株式会社ソープ｜東京都渋谷区渋谷3-2-1北国ビル4階 〒150

㈱ソープ
グラフィックデザイン
SOAP INC.
Graphic Design
AD, D:Takeharu Tanaka

EDWARD GOTTSCHALL
VICE CHAIRMAN
EDITOR OF U&lc

2 HAMMARSKJOLD PLAZA, NEW YORK, NY 10017, (212) 371-0699

タイプフェィス・デザイン
INTERNATIONAL TYPEFACE CORPORATION
Typeface Design
AD, D:Herb Lubalin
T:Tom Carnase

STUDIO BEAM CO.,LTD.

KIKUO TSUJI

STUDIO BEAM CO.,LTD.

HEAD STUDIO　SANBAN BLD. 1-21 3-CHOME, KAWAGUCHI, NISHI-KU OSAKA, JAPAN.
TEL.06-584-3678 FAX.06-584-3679
ESAKA STUDIO 36-29 2-CHOME, TARUMICHO, SUITA
TEL.06-337-6321 FAX.06-337-6322

㈱スタジオビーム
写真
STUDIO BEAM CO.,LTD.
Photography
D:Rie Kikkawa
I:Kiyoshi Tada

Comunication
Coordination
Creation
Culture
Core

さんく・せ

アナウンサー
黒田　善孝
YOSHITAKA KURODA

〒659 芦屋市緑町2-1-102
Tel.0797·23·0044
Fax.0797·23·4545

さんく・せ
アナウンス・クラブ
5C
Announcer's Club
D:Yasuko Kawate
DF:Hi-Fi Company Ltd.

代表取締役社長
representative director, president
楠城信輔
Nobusuke Nanjo

株式会社エイチ・アイ・ディー・アイ 〒108 東京都港区白金台5-5-2マンション白金苑205
HOSPITAL IDENTITY DEVELOPMENT INSTITUTE INC.
205 Mansion Shiroganeen, 5-5-2 Shiroganedai, Minato-ku, Tokyo, 108 Japan. TEL 03-442-7531

㈱エイチ・アイ・ディーアイ
ホスピタル・アイデンティティ企画会社
HOSPITAL IDENTITY DEVELOPMENT INSTITUTE INC.
Hospital C.I.Planning
AD, D:Toshihiro Onimaru
DF:Grafix International Inc.

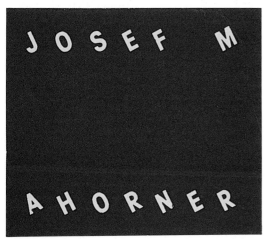
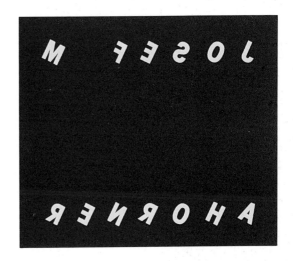

個人用
JOSEF M.AHORNER
Personal Use
AD, D:Harry Metzler
DF:Harry Metzler Artdesign

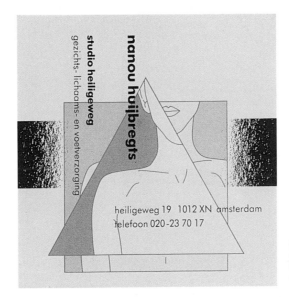

美容室
STUDIO HEILIGEWEG
Beauty Salon
AD, D:Frans Lieshout

㈱イフカンパニー
パッケージ・グラフィック・デザイン
IFF COMPANY INC
Package Graphics Design
AD:Vin Takahashi
D:Masakazu Tagawa

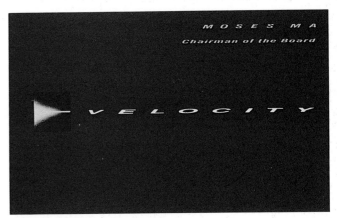

ソフトウエアー開発
VELOCITY DEVELOPMENT CORPORATION
Software Development
AD, D, I:Hock Wah Yeo
I:Chris Kirby
DF:The Design Office of Wong & Yeo

須賀恵美子

タイプ S ＆ S

〒105 東京都港区虎ノ門3-18-6

朝日虎ノ門マンション414号

Phone:03-432-2691

タイプ
S
＆
S

太田美郷

〒105 東京都港区虎ノ門3-18-6

朝日虎ノ門マンション414号

Phone:03-432-2691

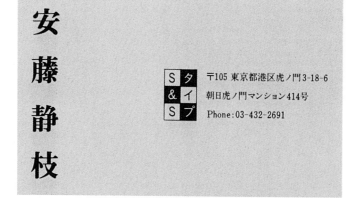

安藤静枝

S タ
＆ イ
S プ

〒105 東京都港区虎ノ門3-18-6

朝日虎ノ門マンション414号

Phone:03-432-2691

タイプS&S
タイプ・オペレーター
TYPE S&S
Typing Services
AD, D:Nobuo Abe
DF:Gong Inc.

須藤政夫
写真
MASAO SUDO
Photography
AD, D:Nobuo Abe
DF:Gong Inc.

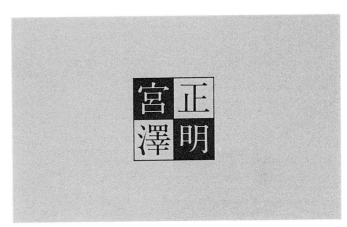

㈲ル・ラッシュ
写真
LE RUSH CO.,LTD.
Photography
D:Masaaki Miyazawa

㈱累
婦人服製造販売
KASANE CO.,LTD.
Women's Fashion Manufacture/Sales
AD:Hiroshi Matsubara
D:Miki Kawaguchi
DF:Projet Cinq Inc.
CI:Hiroshi Itsushiki

鴇田康則
写真
YASUNORI TOKITA
Photography
D:Kenji Oishi
DF:C・S・F・Wood

WIZ ウィズ・トータルプランニング

〒565 吹田市春日4丁目2番1号
緑地公園グランドハイツ210号
PHONE 06-384-5956
ＦＡＸ 06-384-5961

横井 良一

Brad Weaver
Associate Professional

Ko Olina Golf Clu
92-1220 Aliinui Dr
Ewa Beach · Haw
Reservations/St
Administration
Facsimile: (808

ウィズ・トータルプランニング   トゥーズ
空間デザイン   雑貨店
TOTAL PLANNING WIZ   TWOS
Space Design   Grocery Store
AD:Yuki Mikuchi   AD, D:Hiroshi Morishima
D:Ryoichi Yokoi

Ko Olina
GOLF CLUB

J. Craig Williamson PGA
Head Professional-Director of Golf

Ko Olina Golf Club
92-1220 Aliinui Drive
Ewa Beach • Hawaii 96707
Reservations/Starter: (808) 676-5300
Administration/Starter: (808) 676-5300
Facsimile: (808) 676-5309
Mobile Phone: 225-4355

) 676-5300
-5309

Katsuhiko Azuma

KATSUNARI TAMURA

HAN-EI SHICO CO.
NO. 17-7 KOTOBUKI 1-CHOME,
TAITO-KU, TOKYO, JAPAN

TEL. 03 - 841-2089   844-8495

リゾート開発
PAN PACIFIC HOTELIERS LTD.
Resort Development
DF:UCI Inc.

吾妻克彦
アーティスト
KATSUHIKO AZUMA
Artist
AD, D:Hiromi Inayoshi

繁永紙工印刷㈲
印刷会社
HAN-EI SHICO CO.
Printing/Lithography
AD, D:Kai Yoshioka

遠山光宏 **VIVA MAMBO Inc.**
〒151 東京都渋谷区代々木1-27-11
グリーンフラット代々木301
Phone 03・370・4602 Fax 03・370・4613

ビバ・マンボ
デザイン
VIVA MAMBO INC.
Design
AD, D:Mitsuhiro Toyama

関根 **ABE DESIGN ROOM** 清
1-6-23, Shimizudai
Koriyama, Fukushima-ken, Japan 〒963
Phone 0249-38-0358

阿部デザイン室
グラフィックデザイン
ABE DESIGN ROOM
Graphic Design
AD, D, A:Kiyoshi Sekine

代表
杉崎真之助
アートディレクター

㈲真之助事務所 大阪市北区西天満5-16-13 NF高橋ビル5F TEL361-9691 FAX361-9692

㈲真之助事務所
グラフィックデザイン
SHINNOSUKE INC.
Graphic Design
AD, D:Shinnosuke Sugisaki

藁谷映美 おしゃれハウス スカイ
〒130 東京都墨田区江東橋4-27-14 楽天地内
TEL.632-4928

おしゃれハウススカイ
ブティック
BOUTIQUE SKY
Boutique
AD, D:Nobuo Abe
DF:Gong Inc.

高原 宏
HIROSHI TAKAHARA
art director

107 東京都港区南青山 1 - 15 - 22 #305
高原宏デザイン事務所
1-15-22 #305 MINAMIAOYAMA
MINATO-KU TOKYO 107
Phone. 03・404・9963 Fax.404・9727

高原宏デザイン事務所
グラフィックデザイン
HIROSHI TAKAHARA DESIGN OFFICE
Graphic Design
AD:Hiroshi Takahara

林いづみ
企画・編集

Izumi Hayashi

横浜市中区根岸旭台 68 - 1
根岸台ハイツ308〒231
Negishidai Hights 308
68-1 Negishi Asahidai
Naka-ku Yokohama-shi
Tel.045・622・4186
連絡事務所
ホットニュース 403 - 8455

林いづみ
エディター
HAYASHI IZUMI
Editor
D:Takahara Hiroshi

有限会社
小菊編集制作事務所

柳澤明子

〒150
東京都渋谷区恵比寿西2-1-8
曽根ビル402

Telephone
03-780-4885
Facsimile
03-780-4886

侑小菊編集制作事務所
編集/制作
KOGIKU EDITORIAL INC.
Editing
AD:Tsuyokatsu Kudo
D:Toshiyasu Tsurimaki

伊藤佐智子 5'3/10"
Sachico Itoh

㈱シュガー
デザイン
SUGAR INC.
Design
AD:Kaoru Kasai
D:Yoko Inoue

田家阿希雄
イラストレーション
AKIO TAYA
Illustration
D, I:Akio Taya

阿部真理子
イラストレーション
MARIKO ABE
Illustration
AD, D:Mariko Abe

岡本　隆
個人用
TAKASHI OKAMOTO
Personal Use
AD, D:Pamela Virgilio

梶谷デザイン室↑東京都新宿区大京町二十五番地キングダム御苑五〇三号郵便番号一六〇電話〇三―三五八―一七二二ファクス切替可

梶谷デザイン室
デザイン
KAJITANI DESIGN ROOM
Design
AD, D:Yoshiro Kajitani
D:Michiko Arakawa

下谷二助（しもたに・にすけ）仕事場は東京都渋谷区千駄ヶ谷三ノ十三ノ十四、富士ビル四階です。郵便番号は一五一、電話番号は〇三（四〇一）八■六二でファクシミリ共用です。ふだんは午前十一時半ごろ仕事場に入りますが、それ以前と仕事がすんだ後の夜間は留守番電話になります。土曜日もたいがいおりますが留守にすることもあります。不在のとき、あるいは休日などで緊急の場合は自宅あてご連絡ください。自宅の電話番号は〇四二三（二一）六■七六です。

下谷二助
イラストレーション
NISUKE SHIMOTANI
Illustration
D:Nisuke Shimotani

HIDEKI TOGASHI
富樫 英樹

富樫英樹
デザイン
HIDEKI TOGASHI
Design
AD, D:Hideki Togashi

石原章子スタイリスト事務所
石原章子
東京都大田区東雪谷
1-13-18　（〒145）
TEL. 03-748-0056
FAX. 03-748-0055

石原章子
スタイリスト
AKIKO ISHIHARA
Stylist
AD:Isao Sato

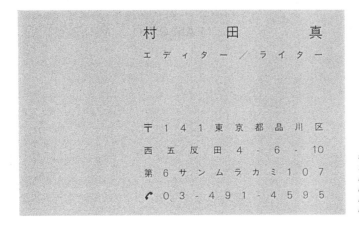

戸田美香
幼稚園教諭
MIKA TODA
Kindergarten
AD：Rutsu Tomita
D：Miyoko Kojima
DF：Ikusūsu・Agora Co., Ltd.

村田　真
エディター/ライター
MAKOTO MURATA
Editor/Writer
D：Shintaro Nakamura
DF：Nakamura Design

㈱小川デザイン事務所
グラフィックデザイン
OGAWA DESIGN OFFICE
Graphic Design
AD, D：Tamako Uno
I：Bolt & Nuts Studio

服部純子
ジュエリー・デザイン
SUMIKO HATTORI
Jewelry Design
AD, D：Kazunari Hattori

石田千尋
グラフィックデザイン
CHIHIRO ISHIDA
Graphic Design
AD, D:Chihiro Ishida

㈱バレンチノ
アパレルメーカー
VALENTINO CO.,LTD.
Apparel Maker
AD, D:Hitoshi Hakuto

小川哲哉事務所
タレント/アナウンサー事務所
TETSUYA OGAWA OFFICE
Talent/Announcer
AD, D:Atsushi Ebina

takada yukiko · manager
高田由紀子
株式会社 正方形
東京都新宿区新宿1-5-3
YKB御苑 〒160
tel:
03 350 0721
fax:
03 350 0723

shinya mitsuhiro · graphic designer
新矢光宏
株式会社 正方形
東京都新宿区新宿1-5-3
YKB御苑 〒160
tel:
03 350 0721
fax:
03 350 0723

sugishita george · graphic designer
杉下城司
株式会社 正方形
東京都新宿区新宿1-5-3
YKB御苑 〒160
tel:
03 350 0721
fax:
03 350 0723

hakamada tomoyuki · copy writer
袴田智之
株式会社 正方形
東京都新宿区新宿1-5-3
YKB御苑 〒160
tel:
03 350 0721
fax:
03 350 0723

kiyohara sachiko · director
清原雄智子
株式会社 正方形
東京都新宿区新宿1-5-3
YKB御苑 〒160
tel:
03 350 0721
fax:
03 350 0723

㈱正方形
グラフィックデザイン
SEIHOKEI CORPORATION
Graphic Design
AD, D:Yoshihisa Shirai

小　泉　英　里　砂

神 奈 川 県 横 浜 市 港 北 区 綱 島 西
2 丁 目 7 － 18 N I C ハ イ ム 綱
島 第 2 － 3 0 7 号 室 〒 2 2 3
☎ 0 4 5 － 5 3 1 － 6 6 2 1

小　泉　英　里　砂

神 奈 川 県 横 浜 市 港 北 区 綱 島 西
2 丁 目 7 － 18 N I C ハ イ ム 綱
島 第 2 － 3 0 7 号 室 〒 2 2 3
☎ 0 4 5 － 5 3 1 － 6 6 2 1

小　泉　英　里　砂

神 奈 川 県 横 浜 市 港 北 区 綱 島 西
2 丁 目 7 － 18 N I C ハ イ ム 綱
島 第 2 － 3 0 7 号 室 〒 2 2 3
☎ 0 4 5 － 5 3 1 － 6 6 2 1

小泉英里砂
イラストレーション
ERISA KOIZUMI
Illustration
D:Natsuko Okada

CAMP&FIRE
CAMP CORPORATION & FIRE MUSIC PUBLISHERS INC.

株式会社キャンプ
株式会社ファイヤー音楽出版
東京都渋谷区渋谷2-3-8　倉島ビル501（〒150）
PHONE：03-400-1920（代）　FAX：03-400-1855

船津奈緒
NAO FUNATSU

CAMP&FIRE
CAMP CORPORATION & FIRE MUSIC PUBLISHERS INC.

株式会社キャンプ
株式会社ファイヤー音楽出版
東京都渋谷区渋谷2-3-8　倉島ビル501（〒150）
PHONE：03-400-1920（代）　FAX：03-400-1855

安室克也
KATSUYA YASUMURO

CAMP&FIRE
CAMP CORPORATION & FIRE MUSIC PUBLISHERS INC.

株式会社キャンプ
株式会社ファイヤー音楽出版
東京都渋谷区渋谷2-3-8　倉島ビル501（〒150）
PHONE：03-400-1920（代）　FAX：03-400-1855

下山典子
NORIKO SHIMOYAMA

㈱キャンプ,㈱ファイヤー音楽出版
音楽プロダクション
CAMP CORPORATION,
FIRE MUSIC PUBLISHERS INC
Music Production
AD, D:Isao Sakai

坂尻　雅
写真
MASASHI SAKAJIRI
Photography
AD, D:Atsushi Ebina

松井桂三デザイン室
デザイン
KEIZO MATSUI AND ASSOCIATES
Design
AD: Keizo Matsui

212 / 966 0511

03/5685 1917

Pamela
Virgilio

Pamela
Virgilio

東
京
都
台
東
区

谷
中
一
、
七
、
二
二

村
山
荘
二
階

パ
メ
ラ
・
バ
ジ
リ
オ

67 Vestry Street

New York

NY

1　0　0　1　3

USA

Murayama-so 2F

Yanaka 1-7-22

Taito-ku Tokyo 110

Japan

Pamela

Virgilio

67 Vestry Street
New York
NY
1　0　0　1　3

212 / 966 0511

Pamela
Virgilio

67 Vestry Street
New York
NY
1　0　0　1　3
USA

Pamela　Virgilio

パメラ・バジリオ
グラフィックデザイン
PAMELA VIRGILIO
Graphic Design
AD, D: Pamela Virgilio

109

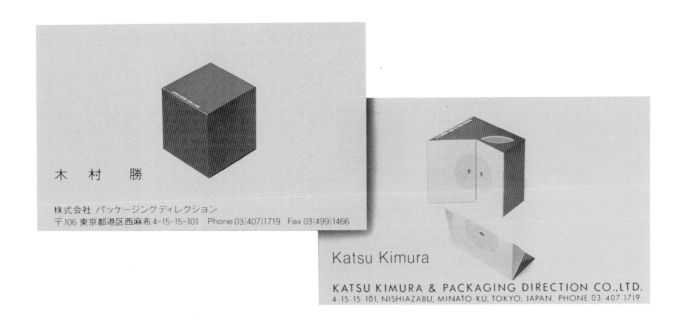

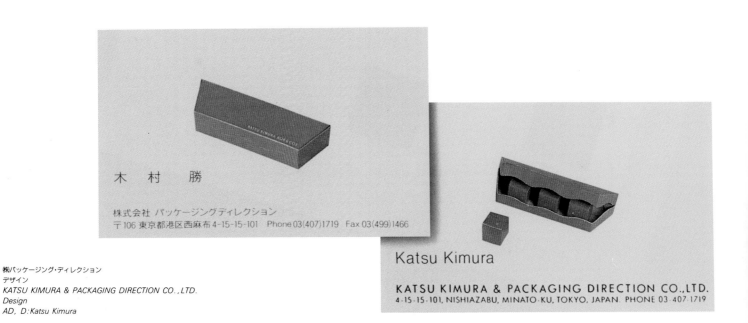

㈱パッケージング・ディレクション
デザイン
KATSU KIMURA & PACKAGING DIRECTION CO.,LTD.
Design
AD，D:Katsu Kimura

KIMIAKI HIROI

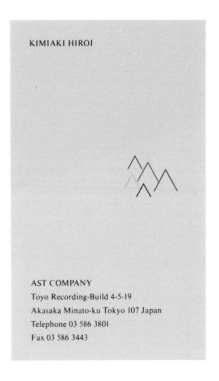

AST COMPANY
Toyo Recording-Build 4-5-19
Akasaka Minato-ku Tokyo 107 Japan
Telephone 03 586 3801
Fax 03 586 3443

KIMIAKI HIROI

AST COMPANY
Toyo Recording-Build 4-5-19
Akasaka Minato-ku Tokyo 107 Japan
Telephone 03 586 3801
Fax 03 586 3443

KIMIAKI HIROI

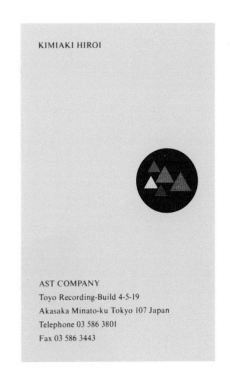

AST COMPANY
Toyo Recording-Build 4-5-19
Akasaka Minato-ku Tokyo 107 Japan
Telephone 03 586 3801
Fax 03 586 3443

KIMIAKI HIROI

AST COMPANY
Toyo Recording-Build 4-5-19
Akasaka Minato-ku Tokyo 107 Japan
Telephone 03 586 3801
Fax 03 586 3443

㈱アスト
美術館/リゾート開発/不動産
AST COMPANY
Museum/Resort Development/Real Estate
AD, D:Hiromi Inayoshi

撮影スタジオ
BCPS
Photo Equipment/Studio Rental
AD, D, I:Laura Silverman
DF:Skolos Wedell Inc.

㈱エヌ・アイ・シー
コンピューター関連企業
NIHON INFORMATION CENTER CO.,LTD.
Computer Manufacture
AD, D:Hiromi Inayoshi

㈱クリエイティブハウス・ディー
広告企画/制作
CREATIVE HOUSE D CO.,LTD.
Advertising
AD, D:Masayuki Kinoshita

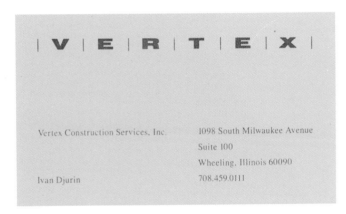

建設会社
VERTEX CONSTRUCTION
Construction
AD:Michael Stanard
D:Marcos Chavez
DF:Michael Stanard Inc.

スキップ富岡
イラストレーション
SKIP TOMIOKA
Illustration
AD:Skip Tomioka

家具店
MANES SPACE
Furniture Store

コマーシャル・フィルム制作
LUCAS FILM COMMERCIAL PRODUCTIONS
Commercial Film Production
AD, D, I:Hock Wah Yeo
DF:The Design Office of Wong & Yeo

Fire Suppression
Technologies, Inc.

1409 Imperial Drive
Durham, NC 27712
919/471-3537
919/383-5324

Stan Parker

Commercial & Industrial
Fire Training
Fire & Safety Equipment
Sales & Service

I K K O
T A N A K A
d e s i g n
s t u d i o

Designer
Taro Matsuyoshi

IKKO TANAKA DESIGN STUDIO
A.Y. Bldg., 7flr, 3-2-2 Kita-Aoyama,
Minato-ku, Tokyo 107 Japan
Phone:03(470)2611 Fax:03(403)6873

Hair & Make-up Artists
No. 301 Nakagin Roppongi
Mansion 6-11-16 Roppongi
Minato-ku, Tokyo, Japan.
Phone & Fax. 03-401-3534

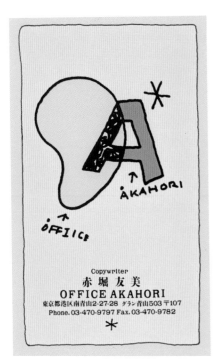

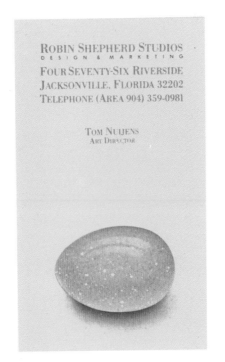

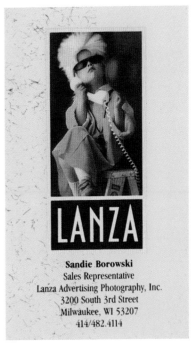

オフィス アカホリ
コピーライター
OFFICE AKAHORI
Copywriter
AD, D:Suteshi Sawamoto

広告/デザイン
ROBIN SHEPHERD STUDIOS
Design/Advertising
AD, D:Tom Nuijens
I:Gerry Bulgrin
DF:Robin Shepherd studios

広告写真
LANZA PHOTOGRAPHY
Advertising Photography
AD, D:Pete Tonn
I:Scott Lanza
DF:Thiel Visual Design, Inc.

伊川英雄
イラストレーション
HIDEO IGAWA
Illustration
AD, D:Hideo Igawa

㈱フォルマインターナショナル
空間デザインサービス
FORMA INTERNASIONAL INC.
Space Planning
AD, D:Takayuki Kuribayashi

グラフィックデザイン
ERIC JON READ
Graphic Design
AD, D, I:Eric Jon Read

イラストレーション
RAMON TEJA
Illustration
AD, D, I:Fernando Medina
DF:F. Medina Design

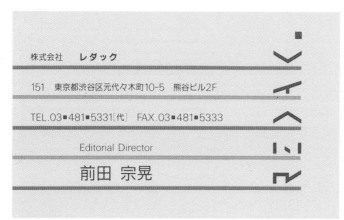

㈱レダック
出版/編集
REDAK.
Publishing/Editing
AD:Kenzo Nakagawa
D:Hiroyasu Nobuyama
D:Satoshi Morikami
DF:Bolt & Nuts Studio

グラフィックデザイン
LLOYD ZIFF DESIGN
Graphic Design
AD, D:Lloyd Ziff
I:Stephen Kclemen

中川十内
写真
JUNAI NAKAGAWA
Photography
AD:Yuji Kimura

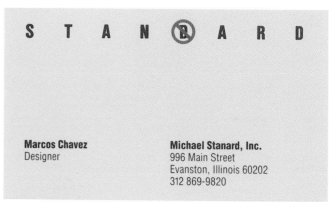

グラフィックデザイン
MICHAEL STANARD, INC.
Graphic Design
AD, D:Michael Stanard
DF:Michael Stanard Inc.

ザ・ステューディオ・トウキョウ・ジャパン
グラフィックデザイン
THE STUDIO TOKYO JAPAN INC.
Graphic Design
AD, I: Yukimasa Okumura
D: Miki Nakamura

建築設計
VAN SAMBEEK & VANVEEN
Architecture
AD, D:Shigeru Watano

市の広報/企画
FOUNDATION PRIMA
Amsterdam Promotion
AD, D:Frans Lieshout
DF:Total Design

デザイン
AXION DESIGN INC.
Design
AD, D, I:Eric Jon Read

精神科医
SIDNEY MILLER
Psychotherapy
AD:Michael Stanard
D:Marcos
DF:Michael Stanard Inc

VAN SAMBEEK
&
VAN VEEN

Erna van Sambeek

Architekten BNA BV
Nieuwe Prinsengracht 33–35
1018 EG Amsterdam
tel 020-22 67 30 fax 020-27 40 74

P R I M A
stichting **Pr**omotie **Im**ago **A**msterdam

daar kan het
amsterdam

Ed. van Thijn
Ere-voorzitter

WTC Amsterdam
Strawinskylaan 505
1077 XX Amsterdam
Telefoon 020-575.3054
Telefax 020-575.3055

werk Stadhuis Amstel 1
1011 PN Amsterdam
Telefoon 020-5522000

Axion Design Inc.

Consultants in
Marketing
Communication
and Design

P.O. Box 629
San Anselmo
California 94960
415 258 6800
Fax 415 459 6816

ERIC.JON READ

Senior Associate

AXION

SIDNEY EILEEN MILLER
RN / LCSW / ACSW

PSYCHOTHERAPY / CONSULTATION

180 NORTH MICHIGAN AVENUE

SUITE 1100

CHICAGO, ILLINOIS 60601

(312) 443-1194

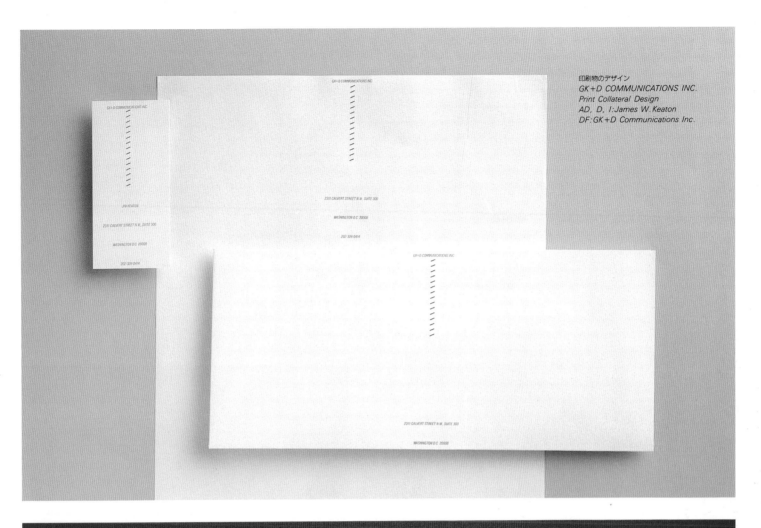

印刷物のデザイン
GK+D COMMUNICATIONS INC.
Print Collateral Design
AD, D, I:James W. Keaton
DF:GK+D Communications Inc.

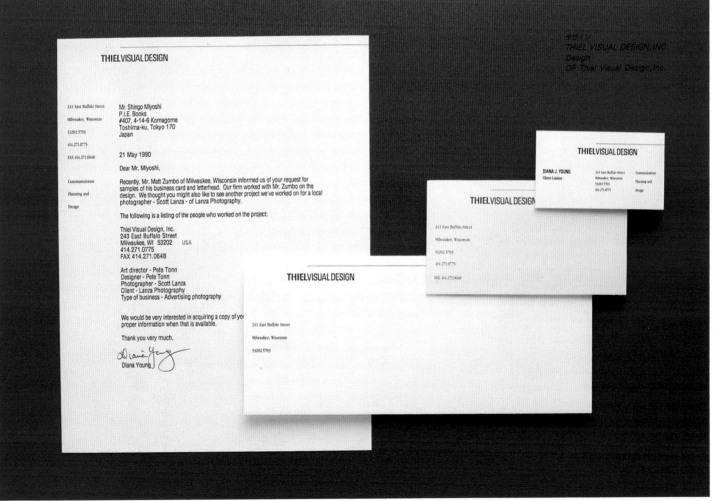

デザイン
THIEL VISUAL DESIGN, INC.
Design
DF:Thiel Visual Design,Inc.

119

マリナ・ド・ブルボン
販売業
MARINA DE BOURBON
Sales
DF:Marina De Bourbon Ltd.

㈱コール・ハーン ギンザストアー
靴屋
COLE・HAAN GINZA STORE CO.,LTD.
Shoe Store
AD, D:Akio Sasagawa

英国家具輸入業
CALEDONIAN INC.
English Furniture Importer
AD, I:Michael Stanard
D:Lisa Finger Hut
DF:Michael Stanard Inc.

東京サバティーニ・インテレスト㈱
レストラン
RISTORANTE ITALIANO SABATINI
Restaurant
CD:Tetsu Kimura
AD:Shuji Toda
D:Mika Takikawa
DF:Kimura Sogei Inc.

英国家具輸入業
BRIAN ANDREW LIMITED
English Furniture Importer
AD:Michael Stanard
D:Marcos Chavez
DF:Michael Stanard Inc.

㈱ブールミッシュ
洋菓子販売/喫茶
BOUL'MICH CO.,LTD.
Cake Shop/Tearoom
D:Hidemi Sakurada
DF:Demisun

ミス パリ
レストラン
MIS PARI
Restaurant
AD:Noboru Kamiyama
DF:W & G

㈲ベリーストックマン
輸入衣料/雑貨卸販売
Bailey STOCK MAN
Import Clothes/Goods Wholesale
I, DF:Art Chambre

ブルーポイント
レストラン
BLUE POINT
Restaurant

シンガポール・レストラン
STRAITS CAFE
Singapore Restaurant
AD, D, I:Hock Wah Yeo
DF:The Design Office of Wong & Yeo

ふーみん
中華風家庭料理店
Fu-Min
Chinese Home-Cooking Restaurant
D:Katsuhiro Kinoshita
I:Tadahito Nadamoto

レストラン
LE COU COU
Restaurant
AD, D, I:Hoi Ping Low
DF:Rod Dyer Group,Inc.

㈱ラフェーテ
インテリア・ショップ
LAFÉTE CO.,LTD.
Interior Shop
AD, D:Taiki Toriyama
DF:Bird Design House

122

ショップ
POTTERY BARN
Retail

㈱ラフェーテ
インテリア・ショップ
LAFÉTE CO., LTD.
Interior Shop
AD, D: Taiki Toriyama
I: Hiroko Toriyama
DF: Bird Design House

シカゴ
バー
CHICAGO (SHINO)
Bar

COMMON THREADS
D: Cathi Howell

遊とい亭
カフェ・レストラン
YU-TOITEI
Cafe Restaurant
AD, D: Keiko Ito
DF: Daiwakogei Kikaku

カメリア メディット
レストラン/バー
CAMELLIA MEDIT
Restaurant/Bar
AD, D: Hiroshi Takahara

BABY
PINK HOUSE

渋谷区神宮前1-8-10 ラフォーレ原宿Part II 2F
TEL.03-408-2072

ベビーピンクハウス
子供服販売店
BABY PINK HOUSE
Children's Wear Shop
AD, D Isao Kaneko
DF Pink House Co., Ltd.

124

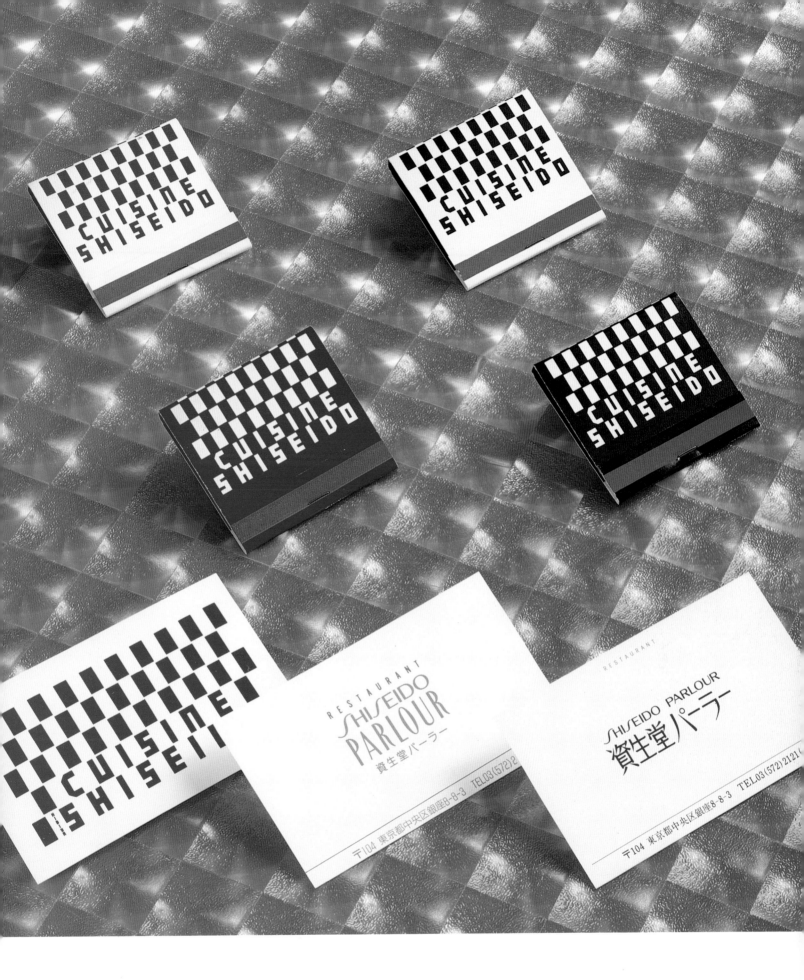

資生堂パーラー
レストラン
SHISEIDO PARLOUR
Restaurant
AD:Isamu Hanauchi
D:Akio Miyake

キュイジーヌ シセイドー
フランス料理レストラン
CUISINE SHISEIDO
French Restaurant
AD:Isamu Hanauchi
D:Akio Miyake
D:Masayoshi Nakajo

SPECIAL
DISCOUNT

INVITATION

ビンゴ・バンゴ・ボンゴ
ディスコ
BINGO・BANGO・BONGO
Discotheque
AD, D:Akihiko Tsukamoto
D:Harumi Tominaga
CD:Nobuo Inoue
I:Bluce Maclane

ビンゴ・バンゴ・ボンゴ
ディスコ
BINGO・BANGO・BONGO
Discotheque
AD, CW:Masataka Sakuma
D:Kazuko Aonuma
I:Bruce Mclane
DF:K & M Ad.Creation

ビンゴ・バンゴ・ボンゴ
ディスコ
BINGO・BANGO・BONGO
Discotheque
AD, D, I:Kazuko Aonuma
CW:Masataka Sakuma
DF:K & M Ad.Creation

OPEN AM. 11:00～PM. 9:00
CLOSED ON 3rd TUE, WED.
NEED AN APPOINTMENT

T.K. IT'S HAIR

7F SHINSIDE BLDG. 22 NAKANO-CHO, UNAGIDANI, MINAMI-KU, OSAKA 542 JAPAN.
TELEPHONE APPOINTMENT 06-245-0789 OFFICE 06-245-0767

ティーケイ イッツ ヘアー
美容室
T.K. IT'S HAIR
Hair Salon
D: Yuichi Nakagawa
DF: Kinema Moon

バイパーチューンドスペース ティ・ワイ・オー
ディスコ
HYPER TUNED SPACE T Y O
Discotheque
AD: Nob Inoue
D: Minoru Tachibana

アクア
レストラン/バー
AQUA
Restaurant/Bar
AD: Hiroshi Takahara

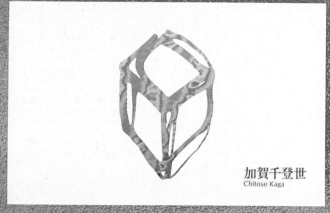

株キューブ コーポレーション
広告企画/制作
CUBE CORPORATION
Advertising
CD: Takanori Aiba
AD, D: Toshihiro Onimaru
DF: Grafix International Inc

サージスタジオ
ビデオ編集プロダクション
SURGE STUDIO
Video Editorial Production
AD, D: Jun Takechi

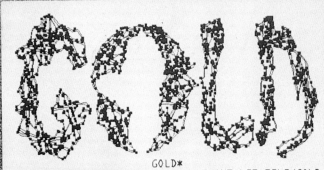

GOLD*
3-1-6 KAIGAN MINATO-KU,TOKYO. PHONE 453-3545/GOLD.
453-5822/LS. 453-4235/YOSHIWARA.453-3481/URASHIMA.

ゴールド
ディスコ
GOLD
Discotheque
AD., D:Koichi Yoshida

ゴールドラッシュ(ロゴ)
ディスコの運営・企画
GOLD RUSH CO.,LTD.
Discotheque Management/Planning
AD., D:Koichi Yoshida

石原章子
スタイリスト
AKIKO ISHIHARA
Stylist
AD:Shinryu Tatsukawa

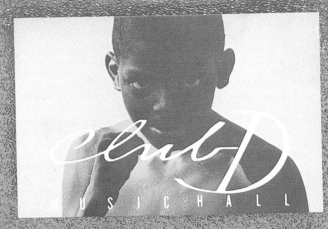

クラブD
ディスコ
CLUB-D
Discotheque
AD:Hiromichi Suzuki
D:Takashi Igarashi
DF:CR Plot Co.,Ltd.

130

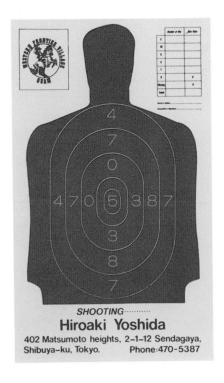

SHOOTING··········
Hiroaki Yoshida
402 Matsumoto heights, 2-1-12 Sendagaya,
Shibuya-ku, Tokyo.   Phone:470-5387

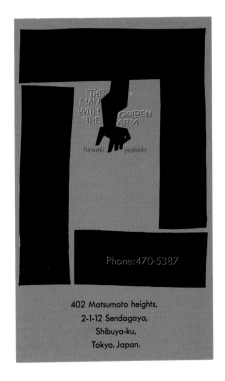

THE
MAN
WITH
THE GOLDEN
ARM

hiroaki yoshida

Phone:470-5387

402 Matsumoto heights,
2-1-12 Sendagaya,
Shibuya-ku,
Tokyo, Japan.

聖林公司
服飾雑貨の製造販売
SEILIN & CO.
Apparel Manufacture/Sales
D: Hiroshi Serizawa
D: Kazumi Uehara
DF: Ford Visual Truck Inc.

聖林公司
服飾雑貨の製造販売
SEILIN & CO.
Apparel Manufacture/Sales
D: Tadamasa Yokoyama

ハリウッドランチマーケット
服飾雑貨の製造販売
HOLLYWOOD LUNCH MARKET
Apparel Manufacture/Sales
D: Seilin & Co.

ペイ デイ
服飾雑貨の製造販売
PAY DAY
Apparel Manufacture/Sales
DF: Seilin & Co.

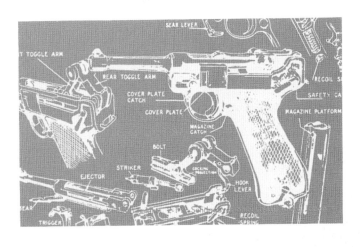

吉田弘明写真事務所
写真
YOSHIDA PHOTO OFFICE
Photography
AD: Hiroaki Yoshida
D: Hironori Yasuda
DF: Pineapple's Studio Graphic

131

スージィ甘金
イラストレーション
SUZY AMAKANE
Illustration
D:Chihiro Shigeyama

コンテムポラリープロダクション
グラフィックデザイン
CONTEMPORARY PRODUCTION
Graphic Design
AD, D:Mitsuo Shindo

シンチャン スタジオ
グラフィックデザイン
SHING-CHANG-STUDIO
Graphic Design
AD, D:Mitsuo Shindo

コンテムポラリープロダクション
グラフィックデザイン
CONTEMPORARY PRODUCTION
Graphic Design
AD:Mitsuo Shindo
D:Naoyuki Suzuki

コンテムポラリープロダクション
グラフィックデザイン
CONTEMPORARY PRODUCTION
Graphic Design
AD, D:Mitsuo Shindo

有限チャンプ
雑貨店
CHAMP LIMITED COMPANY
Grocery Store
D:Yasushi Kurashima

小野寺佐登美
イラストレーション
SATOMI ONODERA
Illustration
AD, D:Mitsuo Shindo

㈱ステレオスタジオ
デザイン
STEREO STUDIO INC.
Design
AD:Tetsuo Fujiwara
D:Sadamichi Hayashi

メロディ ハウス
レコード・ショップ
MELODY HOUSE
Record Shop
AD:Tetsuo Fujiwara
D:Sadamichi Hayashi
DF:Stereo Studio Inc.

有限コガネ虫スタジオ
イラストレーション
KOGANEMUSHI STUDIO
Illustration
D:Chihiro Shigeyama

㈱那覇タワー
ディスコ
NAHA TOWER INC.
Discotheque
AD:Nob Inoue
D:Akihiko Tsukamoto
I:Erick Palen

ゼグノ
ディスコ
ZEGNO
Discotheque
AD:Nob Inoue
D:Minoru Tachibana

ジャバ ジャイブ
ディスコ
JAVA·JIVE
Discotheque
AD: Nob Inoue
D: Akihiko Tsukamoto

サントリー・ビアレストラン・ジアス
レストラン
SUNTORY BEER RESTAURANT THE EARTH
Restaurant
AD: Yukio Ikoma
D: Yumiko Kawasaki
D: Yoshihisa Nagase
T: Mick Haggerty

アーチスト
DEV KUMAR
Tantrik Painter
AD, D: Sudarnshan Dheer

ヘッケルスポーツ
キャラクターグッズ・ショップ
HECKEL SPORT
Character Goods Shop
AD, D: Kojiro Tomoeda

レストラン
TORTOLA
Restaurant
AD, D:Ross Carron
DF:Carron Design

ビスクギャラリー自由が丘
キャラクターグッズ販売
BISCGALLERY JIYUGAOKA
Character Goods Sales

ナイトクラブ
CAFE NEON
Night Club
AD, D:Dennis Veal
I:Monica Krueger

カフェ ミスティック
レストラン
CAFE MYSTIQUE
Restaurant
D:Jun Iida

セーフティゾーン
レストラン
SAFTY ZONE
Restaurant
CD, CW:Makoto Nishimaki
AD, D, I:Yasuhiro Matsui

ウエスト・ウッド
パブリック・バー
WEST WOOD
Bar
AD:Susumu Udagawa
D:Masakatsu Oikawa

上野宏介
イラストレーション
HIROSUKE UENO
Illustration
I:Hirosuke Ueno

プルトニウム
帽子ブランド
PLUTONIUM
Hat Brand I.D.
AD, D:Hirosuke Ueno

カチャトラ
レストラン
CACCIATORA
Restaurant
AD, D, I:Hirosuke Ueno

スーパーセンチメンタル
雑貨販売
SUPER SENTIMENTAL
Post Card/Novelty Sales
AD:Izumi Hiratsuka
D:Chisato Ishimaru

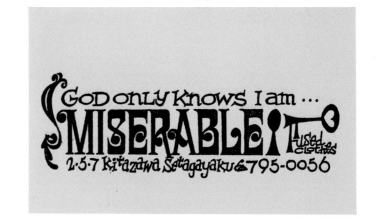

ミゼラブル
衣料雑貨の輸入販売
MISERABLE
Apparel Import/Sales
AD:Manami None
D:Miyuki Morimoto

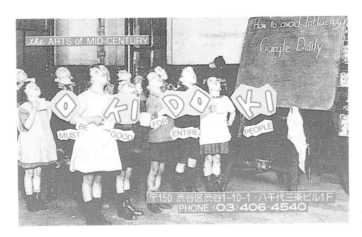

オ・キ・ド・キ
アンティーク・ショップ
O-KI-DO-KI
Antique Shop
AD, D, P, I:Katsuhiro Kido

チャイルド ロック
スナック
CHILD ROCK
Bar
AD:Akira Yamaguchi

スーパーグッズショップ オオウチショウテン
雑貨店
OHUCHI SHOTEN
Housewares Shop
DF:Pineapple's Studio Graphic

古着ショップ
CHAMELEON VINTAGE CLOTHING
Vintage Clothing

コーヒー・ショップ
FABULOUS FIFTIES CAFE
Coffee Shop
AD:Michael Dunlavey
D:Lindy Dunlavey
DF:The Dunlavey Studio

クラブD
ディスコ
CLUB-D
Discotheque
AD:Hiromichi Suzuki
D:Shuzo Tsukahara
DF:CR-Plot Co.,Ltd.

オールディーズ ファン クラブ
イラストレーション
OLDIES FAN CLUB
Illustration
AD, D:Smily Kato

ジーンナッソーズ カンパニー
洋服店
JEAN NASSAUS COMPANY
Tailor
AD:Toru Hirakawa
D:Hironori Yasuda
DF:Pineapple's Studio Graphic

ビリヤード・クラブ
CHELSEA BILLIARDS
Billiard Club

140

LITTLE RICKIE

49½ 1st ave. at 3rd St.
N.Y., N.Y.   10003

212-505-6467

Little Rickie

DOMINATING   CONQUEROR

FAST LUCK   PROTECTION

DIVINE EYE   MONEY DRAWING

PEACE

49½ 1st ave. at 3rd St.

N.Y., N.Y.   10003

212-505-6467

Little Rickie

NTRA. SRA. DE GUADALUPE

49½ 1st ave. at 3rd St.
N.Y., N.Y.   10003

212-505-6467

BIG NOSE

Little Rickie

49½ 1st ave. at 3rd St.

212-505-6467   N.Y., N.Y.

 fake BEER joke   Giant Tarantula   Hanging Skeleton   CIGARETTE LOADS

LITTLE RICKIE

49½ 1st ave. at 3rd St.
N.Y., N.Y.   10003   212-505-6467

 Squirling Cigar   MORNING BREEZE PERFUME   Whoopee Cushion

For TOPS In Entertainment

Little Rickie

IT'S TERRIFIC
IT ALWAYS HITS
THE MARK

49½ 1st ave. at 3rd St.   212-505-6467
N.Y., N.Y.   10003

ショップ
LITTLE RICKIE
Retail
AD, D: Philip Retzky
I: Julie Wilson

141

RISTORANTE

buono

RISTORANTE
buono

岡本茂男

ヴォーノ
〒107 東京都港区南青山4-25-12 OXY
電話03-5485-6731・6732

ブオーノ
ショップ
BUONO
Shop
AD:Ryohei Kojima
D:Takeshi Abe

142

JOCKE KAITILA

FREDRIC DONNER

SUOMEN VIDEOKRONIKKA

SUOMEN VIDEOKRONIKKA

OBALNE GALERIJE PIRAN

ANDREJ MEDVED

Tartinijev trg 66 330 Piran
telefon: 066,— 73 753

DUŠAN JOVANOVIĆ

Director

Funzi Creative Network Oy
Aleksanterinkatu 12
00170 Helsinki Finland
tel: +358-0-630 600
fax: +358-0-630 700

CREATIVE NETWORK
Funzi

TV HOUSE

ANDERS LINDH

STUREGATAN 58
114 36 STOCKHOLM, SWEDEN
660 27 00   TELEX 113 48 TVH S

ビデオ制作
VIDEOSTYLE / VIDEOCHRONICLE
Video Production
D:Dušan Jovanović
DF:Funzi Creative Network

アート・ギャラリー
OBALNE GALERIJE PIRAN
Art Gallery
D:Dušan Jovanović
DF:Funzi Creative Network

デザイン
FUNZI CREATIVE NETWORK
Design
D:Dušan Jovanović
DF:Funzi Creative Network

映画/ビデオ制作
TV HOUSE
Film/Video Production
D:Dušan Jovanović
DF:Funzi Creative Network

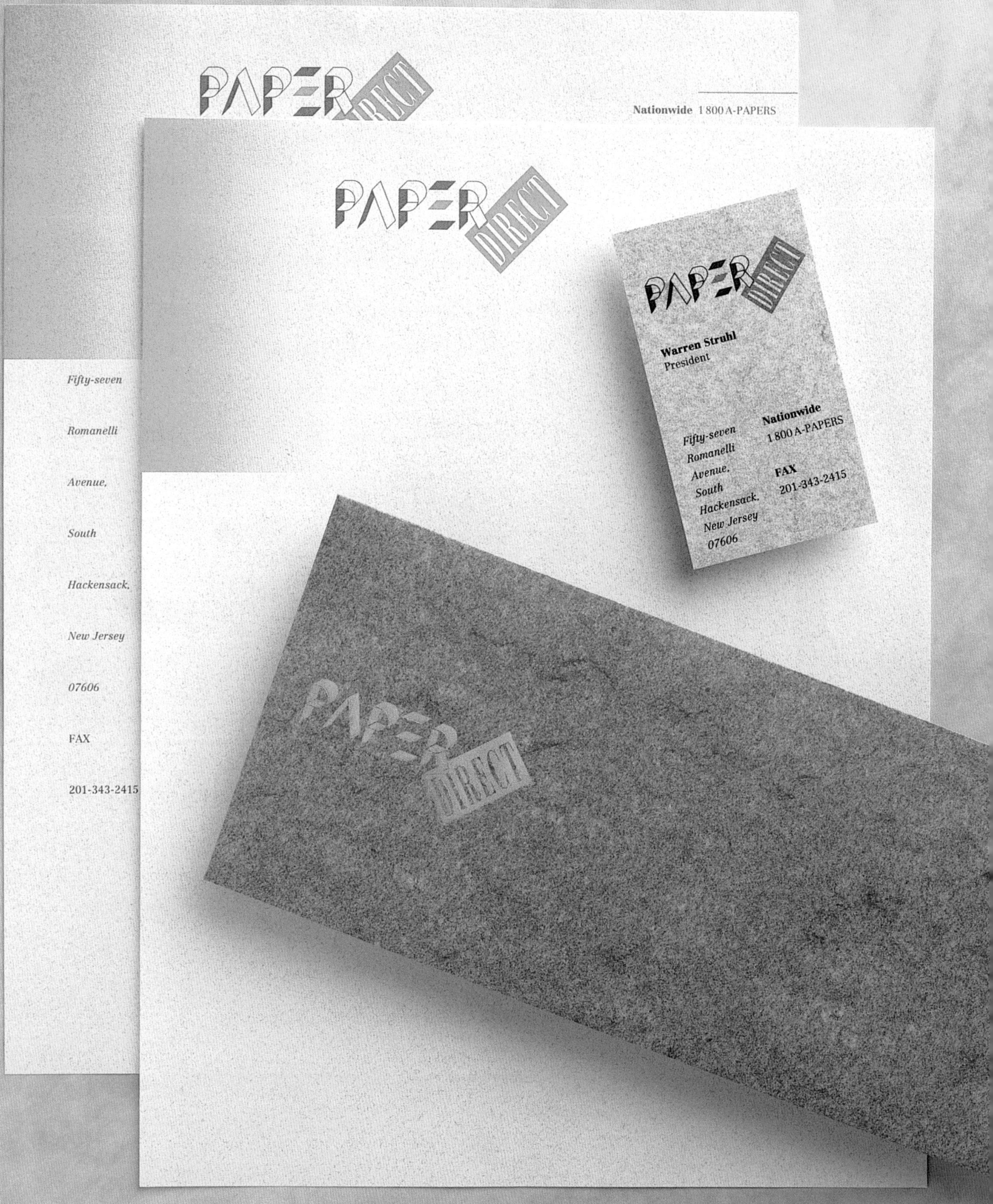

Fifty-seven

Romanelli

Avenue,

South

Hackensack,

New Jersey

07606

FAX

201-343-2415

Warren Struhl
President

Fifty-seven   **Nationwide**
Romanelli   1 800 A-PAPERS
Avenue,
South   **FAX**
Hackensack,   201-343-2415
New Jersey
07606

紙卸販売
PAPER DIRECT
Paper Distribution
AD : David Dunkelberger
D : Mary Jane Broadbent
DF : Weisz Yang Dunkelberger Inc.

グラフィックデザイン
READ & ASSOCIATES
Graphic Design
AD, D, I : Eric Jon Read

オリエンタル スーク
レストラン/バー
ORIENTAL SOUK
Restaurant/Bar
AD : Hiroki Taniguchi
D : Ichiro Tanida

エム・ラボ
美容室
M・LABO
Hair Salon
AD, D : Taro Manabe

145

プロダクションインターナショナル
美容室
PRODUCTION INTERNATIONAL
Hair Salon
D: Yuichi Nakagawa
DF: Kinema Moon

146

陳幼堅

Alan Chan
Director

Sunnie & Company
301/802, 8/F.,
Shiu Lam Building,
23 Luard Road,
Wanchai,
Hong Kong.
Telephone: 5-278228
Fax: 5-8656170

デザイン
SUNNIE & COMPANY
Design
AD, D:Alan Chan
DF:Alan Chan Design Co.

手 相 観
Palm reader

●

日笠雅子

東京都渋谷区神宮前2-19-11 シャンボール原宿302
〒150 Phone & Fax 03-404-1855

日笠雅子
手相見
MASAKO HIKASA
Palm Reader
AD:Noriko Isogai

代表
杉山 正和
Masakazu Sugiyama

岐阜市三番町20 フロムイーストBF 〒500
TEL 0582-63-1186

女将
杉山 美穂子
Mihoko Sugiyama

岐阜市三番町20 フロムイーストBF 〒500
TEL 0582-63-1186

日本料理 すぎ萬
日本料理店
SUGIMAN
Japanese Restaurant
AD: Yutaka Onishi
D: Mitsuyo Okada
P: Takayoshi Sasaki

REIKO OGINO

4-20-11 NISHISUGAMO
TOSHIMA-KU
TEL 03 (91

REIKO OGINO

4-20-11 NISHISUGAMO
TOSHIM
TEL O

荻野令子
漆製造作家
REIKO OGINO
Japanese Lacquer Artist
D: Reiko Ogino

REIKO OGINO

4-20-11 NISHISUGAMO
TOSHIMA-KU, TOKYO, JAPAN
TEL 03 (918) 0 6 4 1

蓬田やすひろ
イラストレーション
YASUHIRO YOMOGIDA
Illustration
D:Yasuhiro Yomogida

蓬田やすひろ
東京都杉並区高円寺南1-5-4-402
電話＝(03)315:0392 郵便番号＝166

蓬田やすひろ
東京都杉並区松ノ木2-19-2
電話＝(03)315:0392 郵便番号＝166

東京都港区赤坂二丁目十六番地六号 〒一〇七
電話／五八三ー二七七八

佳境亭 山上磨智子

佳境亭
料亭
KAKYOTEI
Japanese Restaurant
AD, D:Hiroaki Imai
I:Yasuhiro Yomogida

床屋かなぶん
イラストレーション
TOKOYA KANABUN
Illustration
D:Takayuki Soeda

（天下のさし絵描き）
床屋かなぶん
東京都品川区東大井3の1の10
グリーンテラス木の芽坂203号
電話762の2799　郵便番号140

（天下のさし絵描き）
床屋かなぶん
東京都品川区東大井3の1の10
グリーンテラス木の芽坂203号
電話762の2799　郵便番号140

（天下のさし絵描き）
床屋かなぶん
東京都品川区東大井3の1の10
グリーンテラス木の芽坂203号
電話762の2799　郵便番号140

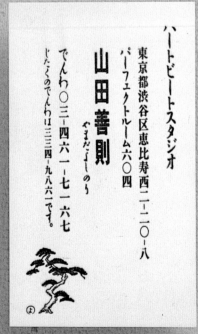

ハートビートスタジオ

東京都渋谷区恵比寿西二‐二〇‐八
パーフェクトルーム六〇四

山田善則
やまだよしのり

でんわ〇三‐四六一‐七一六七
じたくのでんわは三三四‐九八六一です。

ハートビートスタジオ
イラストレーション
HEART BEAT STUDIO
Illustration
AD, D:Mitsuo Shindo
I:Yoshinori Yamada

限りなく
天国に
近い、
ドラマー

福沢　章
ドラマー
AKIRA FUKUZAWA
Drummer
D:Yumi Sawai

OYA·G·DO

ヌマゲン
Genqui Numata

芸術家
沼田 元気

大衆浴場研究家
銭湯壁画美術評論家
温泉レポーター

G N
Genqui Numata
FAREAST
UNDERGROUND
ARTBASE
3 Yarikuri Nagaya, Anone Yokocho,
2-3-7 Mita Meguro-ku Tokyo Japan
TEL.813-791-1845/81468-75-4087

沼田元気
GENQUI

吉田 ツコ
Etsuko Yoshida

沼田元気

FAREAST
UNDERGROUND
ARTBASE
3 Yarikuri Nagaya, Anone Yokocho,
2-3-7 Mita Meguro-ku Tokyo Japan
TEL.813-791-1845/81468-75-4087

国際おやじ堂
お土産百貨店
OYAJI·DO INTERNATIONAL
Souvenir Shop
D:Genki Numata

沼田元気
芸術家
GENKI NUMATA
Artist
D:Genki Numata

極東アングラ芸術基地
芸術家
FAR EAST UNDERGROUND ART BASE
Artist
D:Genki Numata

 菅原 久美

〒204
東京都清瀬市松山 2 － 6 － 19
TEL
0424－93－7796

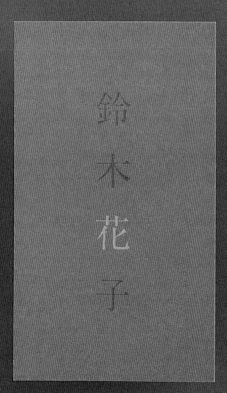

飯盛雅子
アーティスト
MASAKO IIMORI
Artist
AD, D:Mieko Misawa
I:Masakatsu Shimoda

菅原久美
イラストレーション
KUMI SUGAWARA
Illustration
I:Kumi Sugawara

ハナコ
CMのプランニング
HANACO
Commercial Planning
AD, D:Masahisa Nakamura

田村みどり
インテリアコーディネイター
MIDORI TAMURA
Interior Coordinator
D:Koji Mizutani

ビアル・ベロ
ショップ
VALE BELLO
Shop
AD:Ryohei Kojima
D:Takeshi Abe

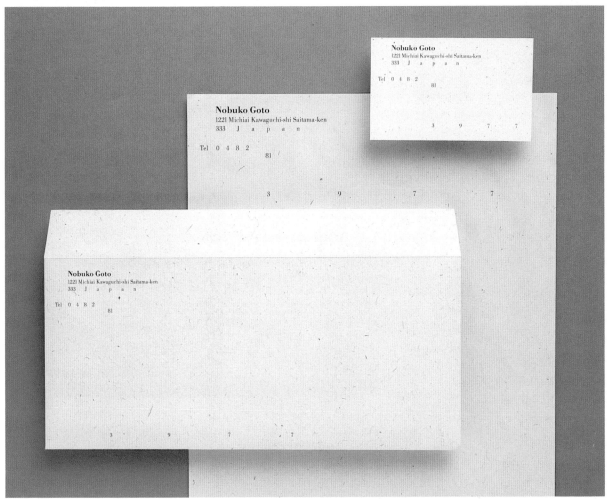

後藤展子
グラフィックデザイン
NOBUKO GOTO
Graphic Design
AD, D:Yoshihisa Shirai

isabelle Dervaux
illustrator

represented by Junko Wong
4-24-7-204 Nakaochiai
Shinjuku-ku TOKYO 161
Tel & Fax：(03)565-0906

ファッション・デザイン
DOMINIQUE AVRIL
Fashion Design
AD, D, I:François Avril

イラストレーション
FRANÇOIS AVRIL
Illustration
AD, D:François Avril

グラフィックデザイン
ZASK
Graphic Design
AD, D, I:Catherine Zask

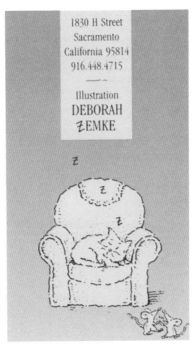

イラストレーション
PETIT ROULET
Illustration
AD, D:Petit Roulet

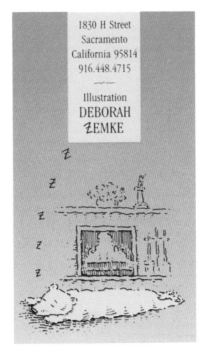

イラストレーション
DEBORAH ZEMKE
Illustration
AD, D, I:DEBORAH ZEMKE

ハルオ宮内
リビング・アーティスト
HARUO MIYAUCHI
Illustration
AD, D, I:Haruo Miyauchi

ハルオ 宮内
LIVING ARTIST

吉祥寺南町1-31-9 Phone.0422-44-1573
ィス Phone.052-951-3918

ＨＡＲＵＯ
NEW YORK
HARUO'S CREATIVE ART FOR YOUR LIFESTYLE.

ハルオ 宮内
LIVING ARTIST

市吉祥寺南町1-31-9 Phone.0422-44-1573
フィス 株式会社ハルオインターナショナル
-17-38 38ビル205号 Phone.052-951-3918

ハルオ 宮内
LIVING ARTIST

〒180 東京都武蔵野市吉祥寺南町1-31-9 Phone.0422-44-1573

オフィス：株式会社ハルオインターナショナル
〒460 名古屋市中区大須4-11-17日比野ユーハウスビル8F
Phone.052-263-4866 FAX.052-263-4948

Sachiko Nakamura

♯107 4-8-7 MATSUBARA
SETAGAYA-KU TOKYO   TEL (324) 5023

中村幸子
イラストレーション
SACHIKO NAKAMURA
Illustration

STUDIO FT

ILLUSTRATOR
ツエ　ムラ
杖村さえ子
仕事場
ZIP160 東京都新宿区北新宿1-30-15
サンハイツ北新宿101
(03)366-2024

杖村さえ子
イラストレーション
SAEKO TSUEMURA
Illustration
D:Saeko Tsuemura

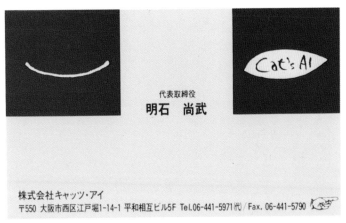

㈱キャッツ・アイ
イベント企画制作
CAT'S AI INC.
Event Planning
AD, D: Toru Hara
DF: Do-it

トレーシースタジオ カンパニー
写真
TRACY STUDIO COMPANY
Photography
AD:Masanori Kato
D:Hironori Yasuda
DF:Pineapple's Studio Graphic

㈱トイズ
トーイズ・ミュージアム/グッズ販売
TOYS CORP
Toy Museum/Store
AD, D:Masayuki Yano
I:Iku Akiyama

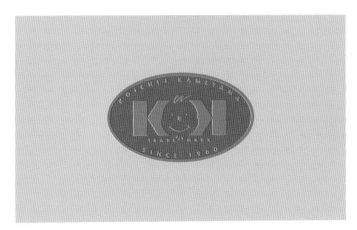

亀山こーいち(宏一)
コピーライター
KOICHI KAMEYAMA
Copywriter
AD, D:Tatsuaki Yasuno

㈱赤井邦彦事務所
ジャーナリスト
KUNIHIKO AKAI & ASSOCIATES
Journalist
AD, I:Taro Manabe
D:Ayako Taniyama

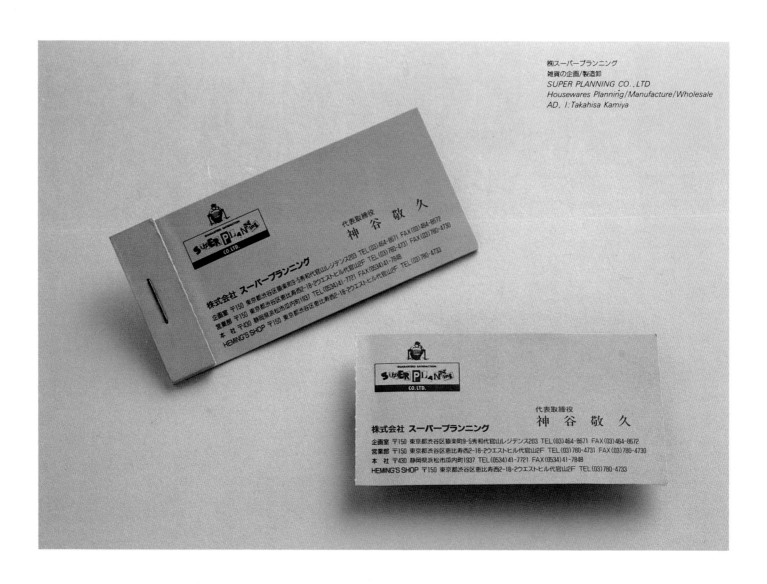

㈱スーパープランニング
雑貨の企画/製造卸
SUPER PLANNING CO.,LTD
Housewares Planning/Manufacture/Wholesale
AD, I:Takahisa Kamiya

artist
HIRANO Keiko

1-25-13-301 Kaminoge
Setagaya-ku Tokyo Japan
phone.03-5706-6548 〒158

○事務所を下記に移転いたしました。
お手数ですが、お手元の名刺と交換してください。

〒158 東京都世田谷区上野毛1-25-13-301
phone.03-5706-6548

平野敬子

平野敬子
イラストレーション
KEIKO HIRANO
Illustration
D:Kaoru Kasai

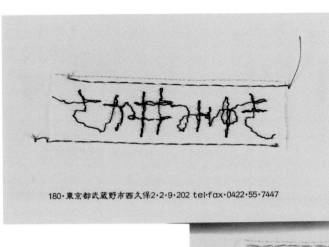

さか井みゆき
イラストレーション
MIYUKI SAKAI
Illustration
AD, D:Miyuki Sakai

180・東京都武蔵野市西久保2・2・9・202 tel・fax・0422・55・7447

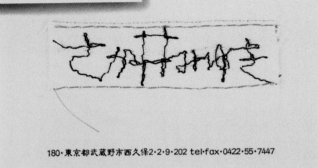

180・東京都武蔵野市西久保2・2・9・202 tel・fax・0422・55・7447

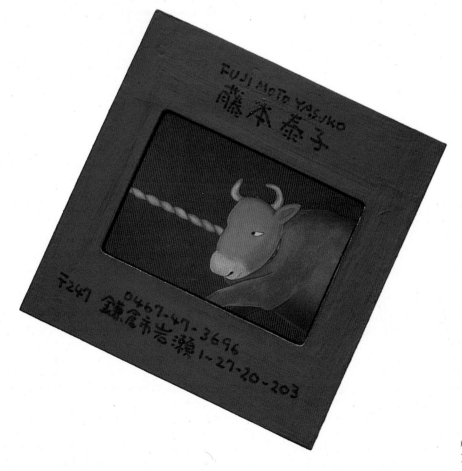

藤本泰子
イラストレーション
YASUKO FUJIMOTO
Illustration
D, I:Yasuko Fujimoto

レストラン
OPERA ON OCEAN
Restaurant
AD, D, I:Harriet Breitborde
DF:Rod Dyer Group,Inc.

パブリック ジェイ
小売業
Public-J
Retail Business
AD, D: Tetsu Hamasaki
I: Yasuyo Ifuku

レストラン
TULIPE
Restaurant
AD, D, I:Harriet Breitborde
DF:Rod Dyer Group,Inc.

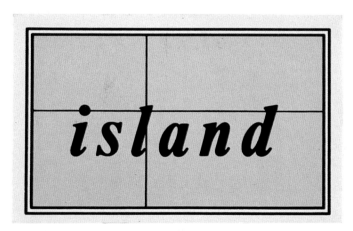

イスランド
輸入衣料販売/卸売
ISLAND
Import Clothes Wholesale/Retail
DF:Island Paris

レストラン
LEMON GRASS
Restaurant
AD:Michael Dunlavey
D:Lindy Dunlavey
DF:The Dunlavey Studio

クラフト・ギャラリー
CIVILISATION
Contemporary Craft Gallery
D, I:Mark Virich

コーヒー会社
PASQUA
Coffee Company
AD, D, I:Eric Jon Read

レストラン
TANGO BISTRO & BAR
Restaurant
AD:Michael Dunlavey
D:Heidi tomlinson
DF:The Dunlavey Studio

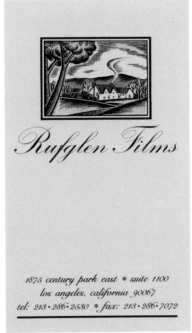

映画制作
RUFGLEN FILMS
Film Production
AD, D, I:Harriet Breitborde
DF:Rod Dyer Group, Inc.

ベーカリー
AMERICAN HOME BACKERS
Bakery
AD, D:Michael Stanard
DF:Michael Stanard Inc.

建築設計
SNYDER WICK ASSOCIATES
Architecture
AD:Michael
D:Marcos
I:Victoria Snyder
DF:Michael Stanard Inc.

CLASSIC GALLERY
SENSUI SO CO LTD

Director
KIKUO OHTSUKA
Altana Yoyogi Oyama 301, 2-17 Oyama-cho, Shibuya-ku, Tokyo, Japan. Tel 03-468-3011
80 Madison Ave New York, NY 10016 Tel 212-889-8726 / 212-663-7507

千疋屋
HARAJUKU SEMBIKIYA

自然がくれた贈り物、丸のままの果物や
果物から創られる多彩なデザートなど、
香り高い世界で、旬をお楽しみ下さい。
テイクアウトから、フルーツギフトまで、
フルーツライブハウス、原宿の千疋屋

FRUIT LIVE HOUSE

FAIR MARYL

Open 10:30a.m.～6:30p.m. Closed on SUNDAY

SUNSTONE-BLDG,1-15-1 HIGASHI UENO TAITOH-KU TOKYO 〒110 PHONE 03-837-5644

Good Appetite!
Neither The Peculiar Nor The Ordinary
Kinetics

PACIFIC MANSION 5-A 10-14 SARUGAKU-CHO SHIBUYA-KU TOKYO
Phone 03·463·2509   Open 11:00a.m.～7:00p.m. Closed on MONDAY

bistro
TANAKAEN
田中園

榛樹水荘
輸入家具販売
SENSUI SO CO.,LTD
Import Furniture Retail
AD: Kotaro Suzuki
D: Kinka Teraya
DF: Quartar Graphics

原宿千疋屋
果実販売／フルーツパーラー
HARAJUKU SEMBIKIYA
Fruit Parlour / Retail
AD., D., I: Eiko Ishikawa
DF: Studio Comtech

フェアメリル
ジュエリーパッケージショップ
FAIR MARYL
Jewelry Package Shop
AD., D: Kojiro Tompeda

有ギネティクス
ラッピング雑貨・ショップ
KINETICS
Wrapping Goods Shop
AD: Yukiko Sakuma
D: Yukari Tai

ビストロ田中園
ビストロ
BISTRO TANAKAEN
Bistro
AD., D: Jun Takeuchi

ジャノメ・ソーイング・アトリエ・テイスティ
JANOME SEWING ATELIER TASTY
Sewing, Housewares Sales
Masato Hayashi
Tasty

アン・リー
ANN-LEE
Housewares Shop
AD: Takashi Kaminishi
D: Akira Nakane

私の部屋 GIFU
WATASHINO HEYA GIFU
Family Boutique
CD: Yutaka Umeki
AD, D: Mitsuo Okada

マクスフリ・バイ・ジュンコ・シマダ
MAXFLI BY JUNKO SHIMADA
Clothing Manufacture / Wholesale

クレモナ
CREMONA
Bar

ヒポス ヴィア サザビー
ソファー・メーカー
HIPPOS VIA SAZABY
Sofa Maker
AD:Takaaki Matsumoto
D:Reiko Nogami

ハードロックカフェ 東京
アメリカン・レストラン
HARD ROCK CAFE-TOKYO
American Restaurant

キハチ
レストラン
KIHACHI
Restaurant
AD:Harumi Tsuda
D:Yoko Inoue

レストラン
CAFE PRONTO
Restaurant
AD, D:Dennis Veal
I:Monica Krueger

宝石/彫刻販売
EASTERN ARTS
Jewelry/Wood Carving Retail
D:Steve Eastern

オム サヴァイ
ディスプレイ業
HOM SAVAI
Displays
AD:Takashi Komiyama
D:Akira Nukariya

旬無国籍料理 ピラルク
ニューコンセプト・レストラン
PIRARUCU
New Concept Restaurant
AD:Senichi Iwamura
D:Mikio Ezawa
I:Katsuhito Itsusaki

南西部美術品店
STICK, STONE, & BONE
South Western Arts
D, I:Jamila Miller

パスタ・ショップ
PRIMO PIATTO
Pasta Shop
D:Barry Suskind

ブフォンバー
レストラン/バー
BUFÓN BAR
Restaurant/Bar
AD:Hiroshi Takahara
D:Ichiro Sogo

ペペロッソ
レストラン/バー
PEPE ROSSO
Restaurant/Bar
AD:Hiroshi Takahara
D:Ichiro Sogo

カンパニャール
レストラン/バー
CAMPAGNARD
Restaurant/Bar
AD:Hiroshi Takahara
D:Mayumi Oka

テックスメックスカフェ・フエゴ, フエゴバー
レストラン/バー
TEX-MEX CAFE・JUEGO, JUEGO BAR
Restaurant/Bar
AD, D:Hiroshi Takahara

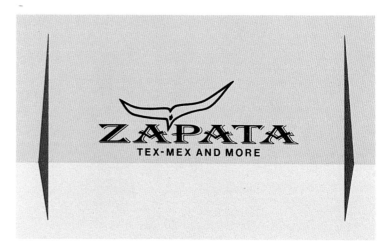

ザパタ
レストラン/バー
ZAPATA
Restaurant/Bar
AD:Hiroshi Takahara
D:Hayahiko Yonaga

タンゴ
レストラン/バー
TANGO
Restaurant/Bar
AD, D:Hiroshi Takahara

グローブ
レストラン/バー
GLOBE
Restaurant/Bar
AD:Hiroshi Takahara
D:Hayahiko Yonaga

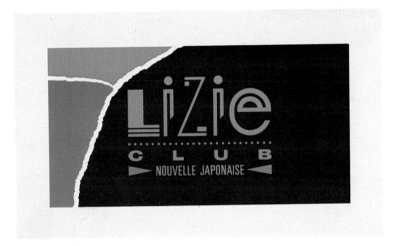

リズィークラブ
レストラン/バー
LIZIE CLUB
Restaurant/Bar
AD, D:Hiroshi Takahara

ニッツア ニッツア バー
バー
NIZZA NIZZA BAR
Bar

ロトゥン
ディスコ
ROTTEN
Discotheque
AD:Hiroshi Takahara
D:Hayahiko Yonaga

ストラクチャーズ
MARK GELARDI
Structures
AD, D, I:Eric Jon Read

レストラン
SPUNTINO
Restaurant
AD, D:Clive Piercy
DF:Rod Dyer Group, Inc.

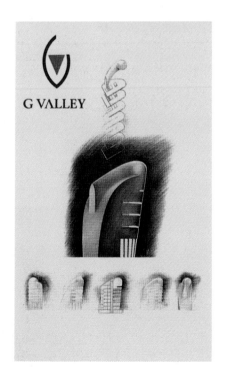

㈱エイペックス
宝飾販売
APEX INC.
Jewelry Retail
AD:Osamu Oto
D:Maki Terao
I:Philippe Starck

文具メーカー
BAZZANA
Stationery Products
AD, D:Vittorio Prina
DF:Visual Due

611 S. Ashland
LaGrange, IL
60525

Children's
Clothing and
Accessories

Joan Fieldhouse
312.352.6082

子供服
JOAN FIELD HOUSE
Children's Clothes
AD:Michael Stanard
D, I:Lisa Finger Hut
DF:Michael Stanard Inc.

印刷業
LUCENTUM
Printer
AD, D, I:Fernando Medina
DF:F. Medina Design

デザイン
NICK BERMAN DESIGN
Design
AD, D:Sandy Pearman
DF:Rod Dyer Group, Inc.

写真
WILLIAM TURNER
Photography
AD, D, I:Eric Jon Read

写真プロデュース
F STOP
Photography Represenative
AD, D:Harvey Appelbaum
DF:The Appelbaum Company

グラフィックデザイン
ERIC JON READ
Graphic Design
AD, D, I:Eric Jon Read

ギャラリー
Vision Gallery,Inc.
Gallery
AD, D, I:Eric Jon Read

UN ON
OFFICE INTERIORS

617.242.8800
Fax: 617.241.7284

90 Cambridge Street
Charlestown, Massachusetts 02129

90 Cambridge Street
Charlestown, Massachusetts 02129

UN ON
OFFICE INTERIORS

617.242.8800
Fax: 617.241.7284

Keith Morgan
Account Manager
Car: 617/930-5847

90 Cambridge Street
Charlestown, Massachusetts 02129

UN ON
OFFICE INTERIORS

ビジネス・ファニチャー
UNION OFFICE INTERIORS
Business Furniture
AD:Nancy Skolos
D, I:Mark Sylvester
DF:Skolos Wedell Inc.

American Corporate Services, Inc.
Computer/Office Systems & Supplies
1-718-854-8607
Leonard S. Goldstein, President

コンピューター製造業
ACSII
Computer Supplies
AD, D:Harvey Appelbaum
DF:The Appelbaum Company

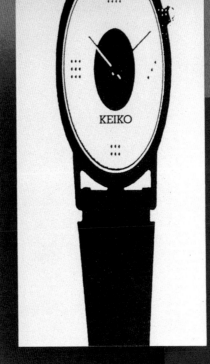

KEIKO

グラフィックデザイン
KEIKO HAYASHI
Graphic Design
AD, D, I:Keiko Hayashi

Keiko
Hayashi
Graphic
Design
3010
North
Main
Street
Soquel
CA
95073
☎
408
475 5179

コンピューター・ストア
COMPUTER CAFE
Computer Store
AD, D:Clive Piercy
DF:Rod Dyer Group, Inc

都市プラン/造園
RATIO
Town Planning/Landscapes
DF:Emery Vincent Associates

Judy A. Friedman

1322 Second St., Suite 24
Santa Monica, CA. 90401
(213) 394-7242

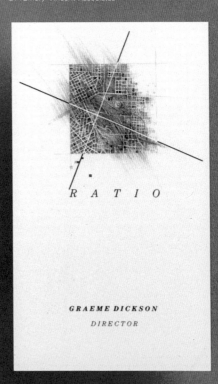

R A T I O

GRAEME DICKSON

DIRECTOR

ダイレクト応対広告
DIRECT RESOURCES INC.
Direct Response Advertising
AD:Dean Morris
DF:Stylism

広告代理店
B. D. FOX & FRIENDS, INC
Advertising Agency
AD:Brian D. Fox
D:Robert Biro
P:Ron Derhacopian

デザイン
MIKE SALISBURY COMMUNICATIONS
Design
AD, D:Michael Salisbuly
DF:Salisbury Communications

C P Y

A & M Records
Akadama (WRG)
Baskin-Robbins (DEM)
Blue Note Records
BodyBoarding Magazine
Brittania Jeans (WRG)
Bud Light (Seatel)
C & H Sugar (FCB Honig)
Camels (McCann/Erickson)
CBS Fox Video
CBS/Columbia Records
Chastain Shadow
Chevrolet (Vic Olesen)
Chrysler Corp.
City Magazine
Coco's Restaurants (DYR)
Columbia Pictures
Criswell Development Co.
D.E.G.
Disneyland
Dorman Winthrop
Embassy Pictures
Esquire
Fats Domino
Filmex
Frances Coppola

MIKE SALISBURY
COMMUNICATIONS
2 2 0 0
A M A P O L A
C O U R T
TORRANCE, CA
9 0 5 0 1
213 320-7660

DATE:

JOB #:

WRITER:

■ MIKE

MIKE SALISBURY
COMMUNICATIONS
2 2 0 0
A M A P O L A
C O U R T
TORRANCE, CA
9 0 5 0 1

MIKE SALISBURY
COMMUNICATIONS
2 2 0 0
A M A P O L A
C O U R T
TORRANCE, CA
9 0 5 0 1
213 320-7660

■ MIKE SALISBURY COMMUNICATIONS   2200 AMAPOLA CT   TORRANCE CA 90501   213 320-7660

Warner Home Video
White Water Falls (W.B. Donor)
XEGM AM 95

㈱ピカロ
デザイン
PICARO CO.,LTD.
Design
AD, D:Taro Manabe

マーケット・アナリスト
LINCOLN W DAY
Market Analysis
AD:Michael Stanard
D, I:Lisa Finger Hut
DF:Michael Stanard Inc.

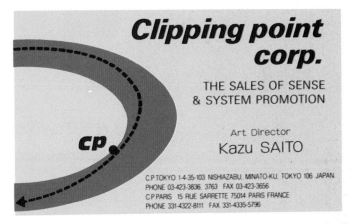

㈱クリッピングポイント
商品企画/開発
CLIPPING POINT CORP.
Product Planning/Development
AD, D:Kazuko Saito

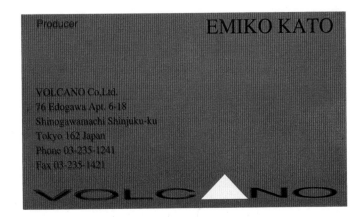

㈱ボルケノ
企画
VOLCANO CO.,LTD.
Planning
AD:Hiroki Taniguchi
D:Ichiro Tanida

ビームス 福岡店
アパレルメーカー
BEAMS FUKUOKA
Apparel Maker
AD:Yasushi Toritsuka
D:Keiko Komada

イラストレーション
MELISSA GRIMES
Illustration
AD, D, I:Melissa Grimes

ランドオフィス
建築設計
LAND OFFICE
Architecture
AD, D:Shinnosuke Sugisaki

広告/デザイン
ROD DYER GROUP, INC.
Design/Advertising
AD, D:Steve Twigger
I:Paul Leith
DF:Rod Dyer Group, Inc.

広告業
ART BRADSHAW
Advertising
AD, D:Scott Mayeda

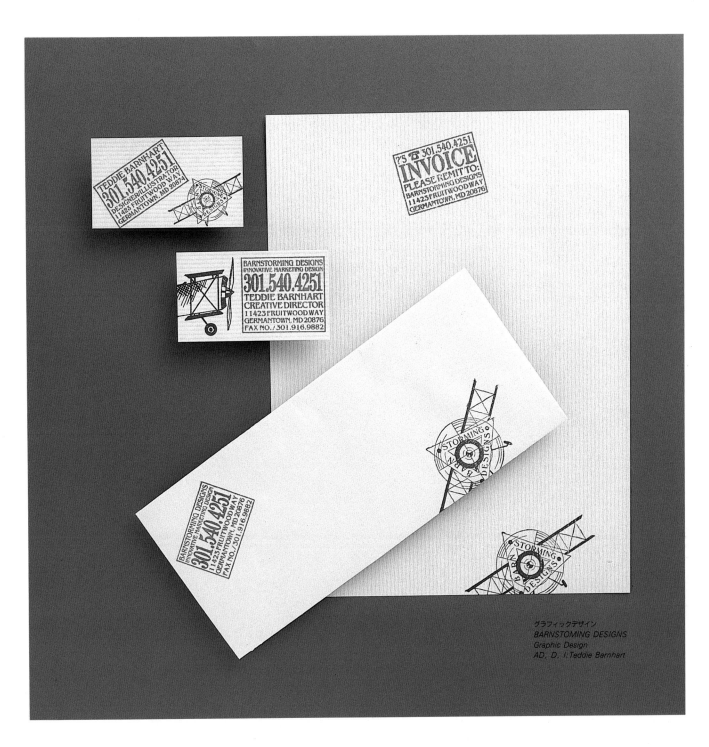

グラフィックデザイン
BARNSTOMING DESIGNS
Graphic Design
AD, D, I:Teddie Barnhart

グラフィックデザイン
CHARLES S.ANDERSON DESIGN CO.
Graphic Design
AD, D, I:Charles Spencer Anderson
DF:Charles S.Anderson Design Co.

ミュージアム
THE CHILDREN'S MUSEUM
Museum
AD, D:Hyla Skudder
D:De Francis

ベーカリー
NONNI'S
Bakery
AD, D, I:Bruce Yelaska
DF:Bruce Yelaska Design

レストラン
CAFE IGUANA
Restaurant
AD, D:Evan Gross

㈱ピセロ
商社
PISELLO CORPORATION
Business Firm
AD, I:Katsuichi Ito
D:Mitsuru Miyakawa

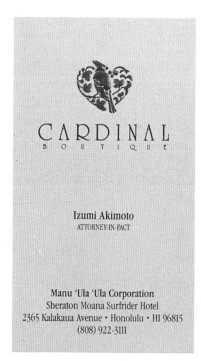

ブティック
CARDINAL BOUTIQUE
Boutique
DF:UCI Inc.

バレエ・ショップ
CLODAGH ROSS WILLIAMS
Ballet Shop

ホテル
SHANGRI-LA
Hotel
AD, D:Clive Piercy
DF:Rod Dyer Group, Inc.

大学
UNIVERSITE DE FRANCHE COMTE
University
AD, D, I:Catherine Zask

バロック・ダンス舞踏団
RIS & DANCERIES
Baroque Dance Company
AD, D, I:Catherine Zask

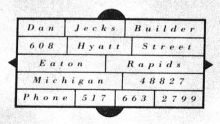

Dan	Jecks	Builder
608	Hyatt	Street
Eaton		Rapids
Michigan		48827
Phone	517 663 2799	

LICENSED | INSURED .

ULU · MAU · STUDIOS · LTD

JANE PAPPIDAS

74 Essex Street • Jersey City NJ 07302
Telephone (201) 432-5001

Susan Baron

m a s s a g e

therapy

212 242 3640
201 866 7707
by appointment

建設業
DAN JECKS
Construction
AD, D Tim Hartford

ULU·MAU·STUDIOS·LTD
AD, D Roger Yu
DF Goodson+Yu Design

マッサージ
SUSAN BARON
Massage
AD, D Pamela Virgilio

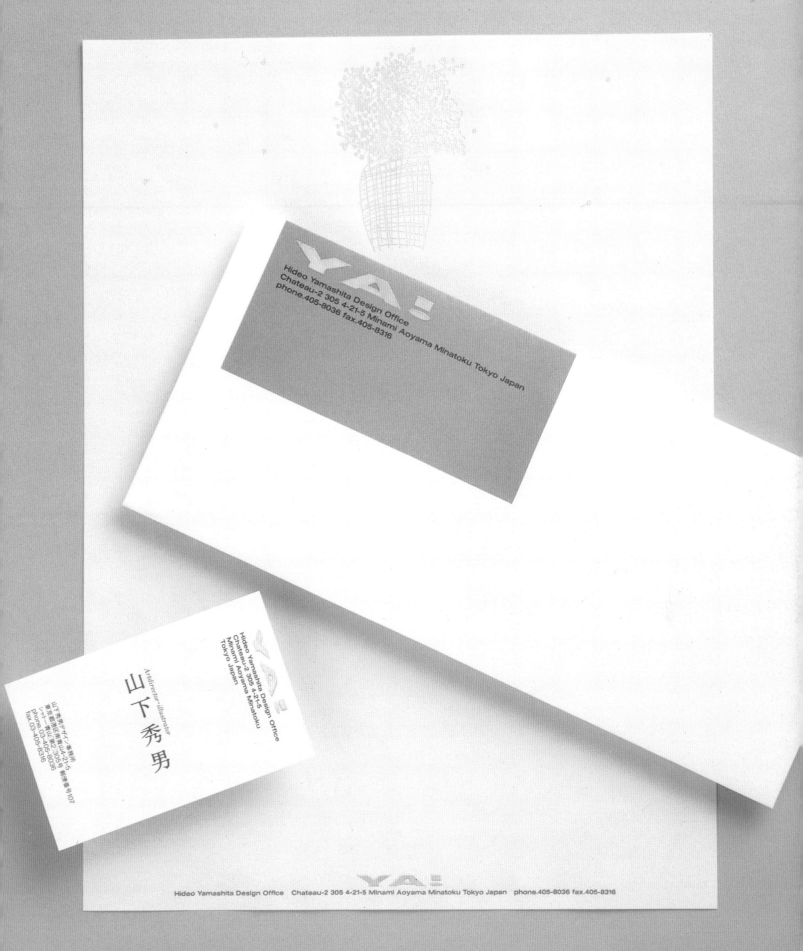

Hideo Yamashita Design Office
Chateau-2 305 4-21-5 Minami Aoyama Minatoku Tokyo Japan
phone.405-8036 fax.405-8316

Hideo Yamashita Design Office
Chateau-2 305 4-21-5
Minami Aoyama Minatoku
Tokyo Japan

Art-director·illustrator

山下秀男

山下秀男デザイン事務所
東京都港区南青山4-21-5 305号　郵便番号107
phone.03-405-8036
fax.03-405-8316

Hideo Yamashita Design Office　Chateau-2 305 4-21-5 Minami Aoyama Minatoku Tokyo Japan　phone.405-8036 fax.405-8316

山下秀男デザイン事務所
デザイン
HIDEO YAMASHITA DESIGN OFFICE
Design
AD，D：Hideo Yamashita

全日本気功協会
JAPAN CHI-KUNG ASSOCIATION
Japan Chi-kung Association
AD, D:Kyoji Nakatani
DF:Kyoji Nakatani Design Office

黒木アトリエ
グラス・アーティスト/翻訳家
KUROKI ATELIER
Glass Artist/Translator
AD, D:Satoshi Urimoto

グラフィックデザイン
SS DESIGN & PRODUCTION
Graphic Design
AD, D:Kan Tai-Keung
DF:Kan Tai-Keung Design & Associates Ltd.

チャイニーズ・レストラン
JADE PAVILION RESTAURANT
Chinese Restaurant
AD, D:Kan Tai-Keung
DF:Kan Tai-Keung Design & Associates Ltd.

John Liu Restaurant Chef
廖沛林

Beijing Hotel Palace Tower
北京飯店貴賓樓

ホテル・サービス
BEIJING HOTEL PALACE TOWER
Hotel Services
AD:Alan Chan
AD:Alvin Chan
DF:Alan Chan Design Co.

SHANG·HAI
上海TIMES

店長
白崎啓子
HIROKO SHRASAKI

〒160 東京都新宿区新宿 3－24－3
スタジオALTA 2F.　TEL03·226·7877

上海TIMES
中国雑貨販売
SHAN·HAI TIMES
Chinese Goods Sales
AD, D, I:Chisato Ishimaru

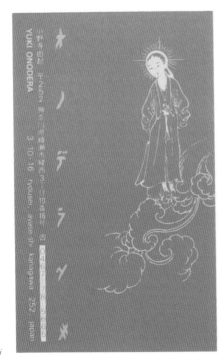

小野寺由起
写真
YUKI ONODERA
Photography
D:Akihiko Tsurumi

晶晶
林子文
Edmond Lum

888 Nelson Street
Vancouver, B.C. Canada V6Z 2H1
(604) 687-8898

Regent
Restaurant

チャイニーズ・レストラン
REGENT RESTAURANT
Chinese Restaurant
AD, D:Kan Tai-Keung
DF:Kan Tai-Keung Design &
Associates Ltd.

広告イラストレーション
MATTE ZUMBO ILLUSTRATION
Advertising Illustration
AD John Thiel
D Pete Tonne
I Matte Zumbo

Suzanne C. Cole

ArteMis
ENTERPRISES INC

PO Box 22326
Seattle, WA 98122
(206) 322-1608

LANDSCAPE WATER AMENITIES
100 EXECUTIVE WAY SUITE 212
PONTE VEDRA BEACH, FLORIDA 32082
904•285•0783

JIMMY GIST

Vice President
Landscape Design & Construction

Vision Care Management Systems

15 Spinning Wheel Road, Suite 10
Hinsdale, Illinois 60521
312.920.1414

Dr. David M. Sobkowiak, O.D.

**Saratoga Film
Corporation**

Beverly Penberthy

200 Park Avenue
Suite 4522
New York, NY 10166
212 972 5170

土地開発
ARTEMIS ENTERPRISES
Real Estate Development
AD:Warren Wilkins/Tommer Peterson
D:Leslie Hoge
I:Karen Sakahara
DF:Wilkins & Peterson

造園業
LANDSCAPE AMENTIES
Landscape Architecture
AD, D:Tom Schifanella
I:Gerry Bulgrin
DF:Robin Shepherd Studios

医療関係
VISION CARE MANAGEMENT SYSTEMS
Health/Vision
AD, D:Michael Stanard
DF:Michael Stanard Inc.

映画制作
SARATOGA FILM CORPORATION
Film Production
AD, D:Debbie Hahn
D:Mark Penberthy
P:Muy Bridge
DF:Playne Design

LION
LION
LION
LION
LION
LION

Armando Tschang
Presidente

Lion Distribution SpA
Via Michelangelo Buonarroti, 7
20090 Segrate (MI)
Tel. 02.2133961/2139375/2138128
Telefax 02.2130330
Telex 312620 OSAMA-I

NAVARRO
Vineyards

Box 47, 5601 Highway 128
Philo, California 95466
Telephone (707) 895-3686

MASSAGE
THERAPY
CENTER
OF
WINNETKA

JOHN G. LOUIS, C.M.T.
DIRECTOR

40 GREEN BAY ROAD
WINNETKA, ILLINOIS 60093
708.446.5700

KARL / PIAIA

CONSULTING ARCHITECTS

2701 Van Ness

#703, San Francisco

California 94109

4   1   5
928.6857

文具問屋
LION DISTRIBUTION
Stationery Distribution
AD, D: Vittorio Prina
DF: Visual Due

ワイン会社
NAVARRO VINEYARDS
Winery
AD, D: Ross Carron
DF: Carron Design

マッサージ治療センター
MASSAGE THERAPY CENTER OF WINNETKA
Massage Therapy
AD: Michael
D: Marcos
DF: Michael Stanard Inc.

建築設計
KARL/PIAIA
Architecture
AD, D, I: Valerie Wong
DF: The Design Office of Wong & Yeo

瀬川真奈美
ヘア・メイクアップ
MANAMI SEGAWA
Hair / Make-up
AD, D: Hiroshi Morishima

北村伊都子
タイム キーパー
ITSUKO KITAMURA
Time Keeper
AD, D: Hiroshi Morishima

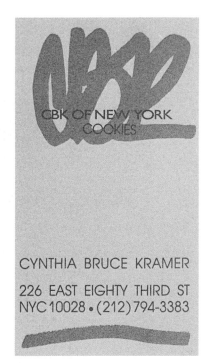

クッキー・ショップ
CBK of New York
Cookies
D: Bill Tsapalis

カード・ストアー
DOES YOUR MOTHER KNOW
Card Store

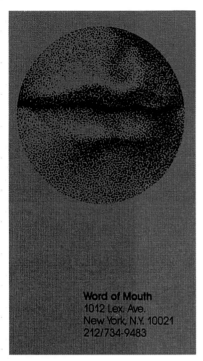

食事のテイクアウト店
WORD OF MOUTH
Gourmet Take-out
D:Roger Whitehouse
I:Conceptual Lithographs

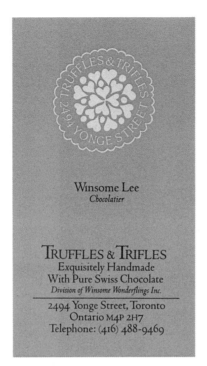

ホームメイド・チョコレート
TRUFFLES & TRIFLES
Homemade Chocolate
AD, D:Raymond Lee
I:Winsome Lee
DF:Raymond & Associates LTD, Advertising

レストラン
SETTE MEZZO
Restaurant
D:Peter F. Dulice

写真
KEN HEYMAN
Photography
AD:Dean Morris
DF:Stylism

ランジェリー・ショップ
LA PETITE COQUETTE
Lingerie
D:Rebecca Apsan

陶器
NATIVE AMERICAN ART
Pottery
AD, D:Tom Schifanella
I:Stuart Findlay
DF:Robin Shepherd Studios

ROBERT H. PERRY
YACHT DESIGNERS, INC.

6400 Seaview Ave. N.W.
Seattle, Washington 98107
206 782 6633

Patrick Walker

ヨット・デザイン
ROBERT H. PERRY
Yacht Design
AD, D:Rick Eiber
DF:Rick Eiber Design

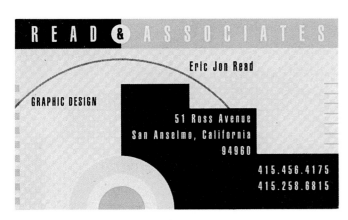

グラフィックデザイン
READ & ASSOCIATES
Graphic Design
AD, D, I:Eric Jon Read

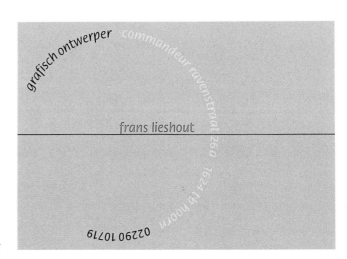

グラフィックデザイン
FRANS LIESHOUT
Graphic Design
AD, D:Frans Lieshout

デザイン・マガジン
ESSE EDITRICE
Design Magazine
AD, D:Vittorio Prina
DF:Visual Due

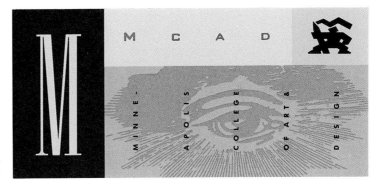

美術学校
MCAD
College of Art & Design
AD, D, I:Charles Spencer Anderson
DF:Charles S. Anderson Design Co.

慈善/政治運動
ADVANCED CAMPAIGN TECHNOLOGIES
Non-Profit/Political Campaigns
AD:Dean Morris
DF:Stylism

建築設計
STUART SILK
Architecture
AD, D:Rick Eiber
DF:Rick Eiber Design

MACOBOUW BV
AD, D:Frans Lieshout
DF:Total Design

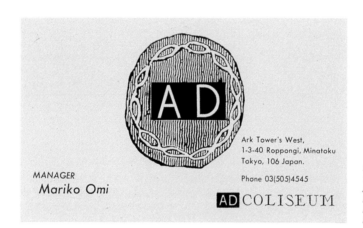

Ashland, Pikeville, Morehead, Hazard, Maysville, Mount Sterling, Newport, Covington, Cynthiana, Paris, Lexington, Winchester, Richmond, Lebanon, Corbin, Middlesboro, Frankfort, Elizabethtown, Danville, Somerset, Madison, Bardstown, Berea, Campbellsville, Louisville, Radcliff, Harrodsburg,

OLD CROW

Glasgow, Bowling Green, Franklin, Madisonville, Cental City, Russellville, Henderson, Owensboro, Hopkinsville, Princeton, Paducah, Murray, Mayfield

オールド・クロウ
レストラン/バー
OLD CROW
Restaurant/Bar
AD, D:Kijuro Yahagi

AD

Ark Tower's West,
1-3-40 Roppongi, Minatoku
Tokyo, 106 Japan.

Phone 03(505)4545

ADCOLISEUM

MANAGER
Mariko Omi

エーディー コリシアム
レストラン
AD COLISEUM
Restaurant
D:Timney and Fowler
DF:Around

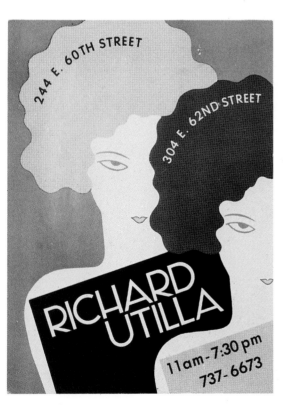

244 E. 60TH STREET
304 E. 62ND STREET

RICHARD UTILLA

11am-7:30 pm
737-6673

アンティーク・ブティック
RICHARD UTILLA
Antique Boutique
D:Richard Utilla

WOOSTER

Kim Shkapich, Curator
101 Wooster Street
DBN Exhibition Space
101 Wooster Street
New York NY 10012
212 219 2790

アート・ギャラリー
101 WOOSTER STREET
Art Gallery
AD:Dean Morris
DF:Stylism

JEAN KARAJIAN GALLERY ART•DECO ART•NOUVEAU

250 E 60th ST.
NYC 10022
(212) 751-6728

アンティーク・ギャラリー
JEAN KARAJIAN GALLERY
Antique Gallery
D:Jean Karajian

デザインスタジオ　あー
デザイン
DESIGN STUDIO AA
Design
AD, D:Kenji Asano

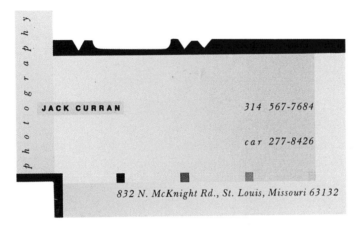

写真
JACK CURRAN
Photography
AD, D, I:David Chiow

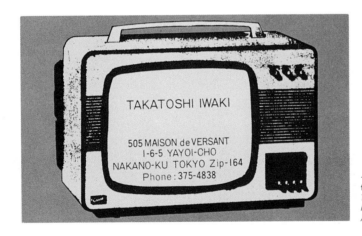

イワキタカトシ
個人用
TAKATOSHI IWAKI
Personal Use
AD:Pineapple's Studio Graphic

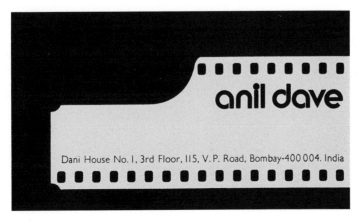

写真
ANIL DAVE
Photography
AD, D:Sudarnshan Dheer

Stationery Coordinator

渡辺琢乎

株式会社 竹尾

東京都千代田区神田錦町3-12-6 〒101　Tel.03(292)3611 Fax.03(295)3980

Restaurant & Bar

ZUNI

1658 Market Street
San Francisco 94102
(415) 552-2522

㈱竹尾
洋紙卸売業
TAKEO CO., LTD.
Paper Wholesale
AD, D:Tetsuya Ota

畠山敏デザイン事務所
デザイン
SATOSHI HATAKEYAMA DESIGN OFFICE
Design
AD, D:Satoshi Hatakeyama

レストラン
ZUNI RESTAURANT
Restaurant
AD, D:Ross Carron
DF:Carron Design

ヤギクリエーション
デザイン
YAGI CREATION
Design
AD, D:Yoshikazu Yagi

㈲ナインハーフ
広告業
NINE HALF INC.
Advertising
CD，D：Yutaka Onishi

㈲松井桂三デザイン室
デザイン
KEIZO MATSUI AND ASSOCIATES
Design
AD，D：Keizo Matsui

勝井デザイン事務所
デザイン
KATSUI DESIGN OFFICE INC.
Design
AD: Mitsuo Katsui

PEIPERS+KOJEN

IRENE KOJEN

───────────

1023 LEXINGTON AVE
(BETW 73RD & 74TH STS)
NEW YORK NY 10021
TEL 212-744-1047

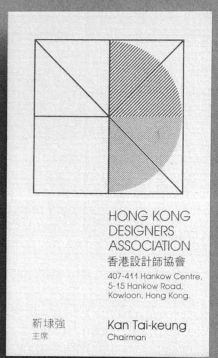

HONG KONG
DESIGNERS
ASSOCIATION
香港設計師協會

407-411 Hankow Centre,
5-15 Hankow Road,
Kowloon, Hong Kong.

靳埭強
主席

Kan Tai-keung
Chairman

With Compliments of

Sudarshan Dheer

10, Sind Chambers
S. Bhagat Singh Road Colaba
Bombay-400 005 – India

Rolf N. Bax
partner

Paardenhoeve 80
3992 PK Houten
Tel 03403 - 77677
Fax 03403 - 80711

assessment centers

Bax Nyst & Zwartkruis

家具/アクセサリー店
PEIPERS+KOJEN
Home Furnishings/Accessories
AD:Flolence Zabick

香港デザイナー協会
HONG KONG DESIGNERS ASSOCIATION
Hong Kong Based Association for Local Designers
AD, D:Kan Tai-Keung
DF:Kan Tai-Keung Design & Associates Ltd.

グラフィックデザイン
SUDARSHAN DHEER
Graphic Design
AD, D:Sudarshan Dheer

アセスメント・センター
BAY NYST & ZWARTKRUIS
Assessment Centers
AD, D:Frans Lieshout
DF:Total Design

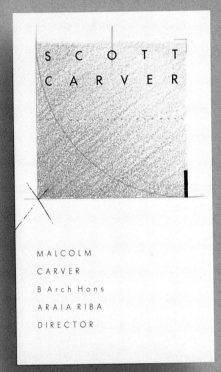

S C O T T
C A R V E R

MALCOLM
CARVER
B Arch Hons
ARAIA RIBA
DIRECTOR

建築設計
SCOTT CARVER
Architecture
DF:Emery Vincent Associates

John de Vries

X Vier
Oosteinde 173 **a**
2611 VD Delft
Postbus 132
2250 AC Voorschoten
Telefoon (015) 14 19 21
Telefax (015) 13 80 53

X4
AD, D:Robert van Rixtel
DF:Studio Henk de Vries

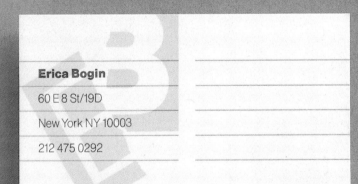

Erica Bogin

60 E 8 St/19D

New York NY 10003

212 475 0292

コラージュ・アーチスト
ERICA BOGIN
Collage Artist
AD, D:Pamela Virgilio

建築マネージメント
THE KLINKAM COMPANY
Construction Management
AD, D:Jack Anderson
D, I:Jani Drewfs
DF:Hornall Anderson Design Works

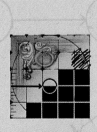

Craig J. Klinkam

Construction
Management

735 Skinner Building
Fifth Avenue
Seattle, WA
98101
(206) 624-9735

THE KLINKAM
COMPANY

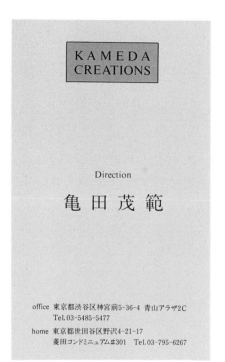

桑山弥志郎
建築設計
YASHIRO KUWAYAMA
Architecture
AD, D:Yasaburo Kuwayama

カメダクリエイションズ
デザイン/写真
KAMEDA CLEATIONS
Design/Photography
AD, D:Sigenori Kameda

㈱小松ストアー
小売業
KOMATSU STORE CO.,LTD.
Retail Business
AD:Keisuke Nagatomo
D:Takashi Nomura
I:Seitaro Kuroda
DF:K₂

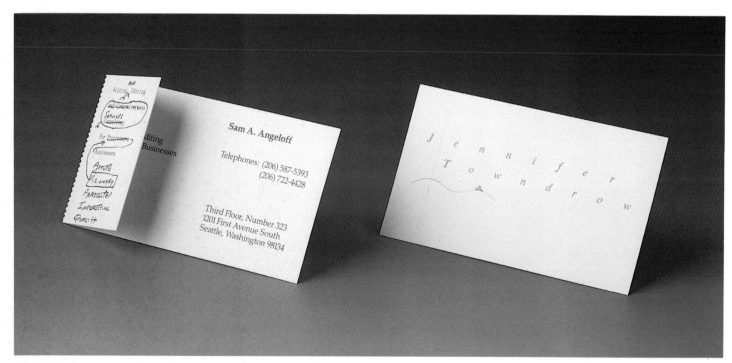

コピーライター
SAM ANGELOFF
Copywriter
AD, D:Rick Eiber
DF:Rick Eiber Design

ジャーナリスト
JENNIFER TOWNDROW
Journalist
DF:Emery Vincent Associates

衣料品店
GEORGIOU
Clothing Store
AD, D:Ross Carron
DF:Carron Design

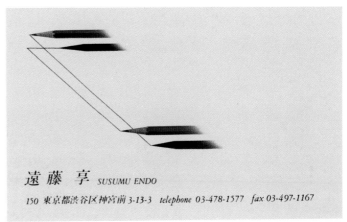

遠藤 亭
グラフィックデザイン
SUSUMU ENDO
Graphic Design
AD, D, P:Susumu Endou
青山見本帖より

㈲アラキ クリエイティブ ブティック
デザイン
ARAKI CREATIVE BOUTIQUE
Design
AD, D:Masato Araki

沢山生也デザイン室
グラフィックデザイン
SEIYA SAWAYAMA DESIGN ROOM
Graphic Design
AD, D:Seiya Sawayama

写真
JIM LASER
Photography
AD, D:Jack Anderson
D:Raymond Terada
I:NA
DF:Hornall Anderson Design Works

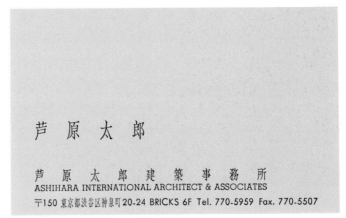

芦原太郎建築事務所
建築設計
ASHIHARA INTERNATIONAL ARCHITECT & ASSOCIATES
Architecture
AD, D:Taro Ashihara

RIKUYO-SHA INTER-MEDIA INC.
2nd Toko Bldg. No.34-15, 1-chome
Shinjuku, Shinjuku-ku, Tokyo, Japan
Tel 03-356-0331 Fax 03-356-0744

PRESIDENT
MITSUSHI TAGUCHI

RIKUYO-SHA INTER-MEDIA, INC.

2nd. Toko Bldg. No. 34-15,
1-chome, Shinjuku, Shinjuku-ku, Tokyo 160 Japan
Tel.03-356-0331 Fax.03-356-0744

RIKUYO-SHA INTER-MEDIA INC.
2nd Toko Bldg. No.34-15, 1-chome
Shinjuku, Shinjuku-ku, Tokyo, Japan
Tel 03-356-0331 Fax 03-356-0744

株式会社リム「六耀社インターメディア」
〒160 東京都新宿区新宿1-34-15
第二東興ビル4階
Tel 03-356-0331(代表) Fax 03-356-0744

株式会社リム「六耀社インターメディア」
〒160 東京都新宿区新宿1-34-15
第二東興ビル4階
Tel 03-356-0331(代表) Fax 03-356-0744

㈱リム
出版/企画
RIKUYO-SHA INTER-MEDIA
Publishing/Planning
AD, D:Yuji Dairokuno

㈱インテグレ
システム開発
INTEGRE CORPORATION
Systems Development
AD:Katsuichi Ito
D:Katsumi Miyasaka

通訳
JEANETTE A. TAUDIN CHABOT
Translation
AD, D:Shigeru Watano

キャンプ場/コテージ経営
INTERLEISURE
Leisure Bungalows & Parks Operation
AD, D:Frans Lieshout
DF:Total Design

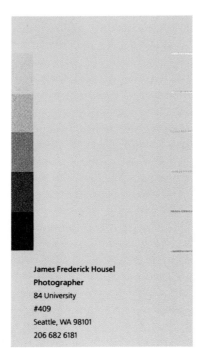

長谷川宏
コピーライター
HIROSHI HASEGAWA
Copywriter
AD:Hiroshi Hasegawa
D:Katsuhiko Narisawa

写真
JAMES FREDERICK HOUSEL
Photography
AD, D:Jack Anderson
D:Raymond Terada
I:NA
DF:Hornall Anderson Design Works

㈱フロス
グラフィックデザイン
FROS INC.
Graphic Design
AD, D:Hiromi Inayoshi

WEB企画室
季刊誌編集スタジオ
WEB
Magazine Editing
D:Akihiko Tsukamoto

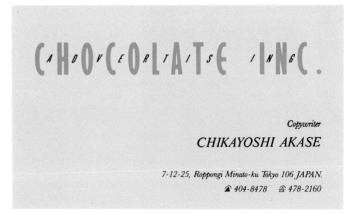

㈱チョコレート
広告企画/制作
CHOCOLATE INC.
Advertising
CD:Toshiro Suzuki
D:Takaaki Mizuno

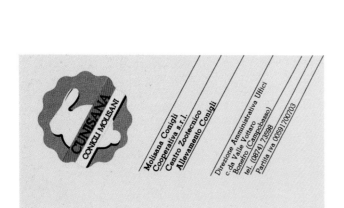

兎の飼育
MOLISANA CONGLI
Rabbit Breeding
AD, D, I:Graziano Uillani

エヌ・スタジオ
グラフィックデザイン
N・STUDIO
Graphic Design
D:Nobuya Sato

㈱アイ・エフ・プランニング
企画/デザイン
I. F. PLANNING INC.
Planning/Design
D:Yukichi Takada

旅行代理店
ASSOCIAZIONE REGIONALE COOPERATIVE TURISTICHE
Tourist Agency Association
AD, D, I:Fabio Adranno

葛西泰行
グラフィックデザイン
YASUYUKI KASAI
Graphic Design
AD, D, A:Yasuyuki Kasai

北川佳子デザインスタジオ
デザイン
YOSHIKO KITAGAWA DESIGN STUDIO
Design
AD, D:Tetsuya Ota

雲母社
音楽プロダクション
KIRARASHA
Music Production
AD, D:Mitsuo Shindo

Waters
デザイン
Waters
Design
AD, D:Yoshihiro Madachi

㈱ラフェーテ
インテリア・ショップ
LAFÉTE CO.,LTD.
Interior Shop
AD, D:Taiki Toriyama
DF:Bird Design House

アクターズプロモーション・A-LINE
タレント・プロダクション
ACTORS PROMOTION・A-LINE
Talent Production
AD, D:Nobukazu Iida

ジュエリー・サロン
FACERE JEWELRY ART
Jewelry Salon
AD, D:Jack Anderson
D:Juliet Shen
I:Bruce Hale
DF:Hornall Anderson Design Works

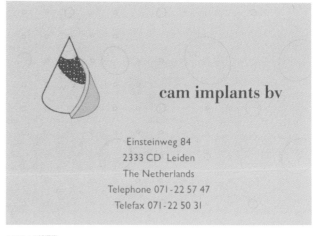

セラミック補綴術
CAM IMPLANTS
Ceramic Prostheses
AD, D:Frans Lieshout
DF:Total Design

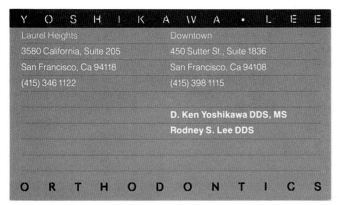

歯列矯正医
YOSHIKAWA DDS/LEE DDS
Orthodontics
AD, D, I:Valerie Wong
DF:The Design Office of Wong & Yeo

㈱シー・ディー
建築設計・コンサルティング
CD INC.
Architectural Consulting
AD, D:Hiromi Inayoshi

日ス アート㈱
金属工芸品/アートデザイン販売
NISSU ART
Metal Crafts Design/Sales
AD:Kenzo Nakagawa
D:Hiroyasu Nobuyama
DF:NDC Graphics

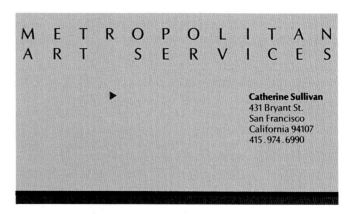

アートサービス
METROPOLITAN ART SERVICES
Art Service
AD, D, I:Eric Jon Read

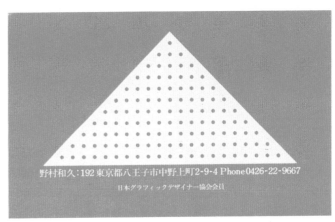

家具店
ARC AMERICA
Furniture Store
AD, D:Tom Schifanella
DF:Robin Shepherd Studios

野村和久
デザイン
KAZUYA NOMURA
Design
AD, D:Kazuhisa Nomura

セス・アソシエイツ
インテリア・デザイン
SES ASSOCIATES
Interior Design
AD, D:Hiroki Taniguchi

管弦楽団
*KONINKLIJK CONCERTGEBOUW
ORKEST*
Orchestra
AD, D:Robert van Rixtel
DF:Total Design

フランチャイズ開発
DRS A.KOELEWIJN
Franchise Development
AD, D:Robert van Rixtel
DF:Studio Henk de Vries

ダンス・スクール
CHOREA
Dance School
AD：Graziano Villani
D：Mara Gessi

レストラン
CUCINA! CUCINA!
Restaurant
AD, D, I：Tim Girvin
DF：Tim Girvin Design, Inc.

レストラン
SUGAR REEF
Restaurant

サイクル・ショップ
CITY CYCLES
Bicycle Shop
D, I：K. Haring

Stylism
307 East 6th St
NY NY 10003
212 420 0673

Dean Morris

Stylism

Stylism
307 East 6th St
NY NY 10003
212 420 0673

S

Stylism

307 East 6th St
NY NY 10003

グラフィックデザイン
STYLISM
Graphic Design
AD : Dean Morris
DF : Stylism

クリーニング会社
SEDIC
Cleaning
AD, D : Hands-George Lang

102 SAINT MARKS PLACE
NEW YORK, NY 10009
212 979-1005

102 SAINT MARKS PLACE
NEW YORK, NY 10009
212 979-1005

婦人帽子店
LOLA
Millinery
AD:Steve Isoz
I:Diana Huff

ITALIAN RESTAURANT
IONONSO
2-17-12 JIYUGAOKA MEGURO-KU TOKYO
TEL. 03-723-8155

イタリアンレストラン イオノンソ
イタリアン・レストラン
ITALIAN RESTAURANT IONONSO
Italian Restaurant
D:Hisashi Hamada

Ray Bari Pizza

"The Only Pizza Worthy of it's Family Name"
Since 1973

ピザ・レストラン
RAY BARI PIZZA
Pizza Restaurant

カリフォルニアワイン協会
ワイン協会
CARIFORNIA WINE LOVERS
Wine Association
AD:Hiroshi Kojitani
D:Irie Kensuke

ライター
CREATIVE PROSE
Writer
AD, D, I:David Chiow

イタリアン・レストラン
DA ALFRED RISTAURANTE
Italian Restaurant
AD, D:Hands-George Lang

レストラン
PIG HEAVEN
Restaurant

化粧品会社
NATALIE JANE
Skin Care Products
AD, D:Dennis Veal
I:Carolyn Morgan

色彩研究所
LIGHTWAVES
Color Laboratory
AD, D:Dennis Veal
I:John Morris

北海男山・田酒・喜久泉・駒泉・菊駒・
日の丸・秀よし・七福神・南部美人・岩
伏見男山・蔵王・出羽桜・初孫・大山・栄光富士・住吉・米鶴・金紋会津・末広
栄川・郷乃譽・一人娘・澤姫・四季桜・大英勇・東力士・東薫・木戸泉・谷桜
大冠・真澄・福無量・真稜・越の華・麒麟山・菊水・吉乃川・清泉・白瀧・〆張鶴
満寿泉・立山・北洋・天狗舞・手取川・菊姫・竹葉・雲乃井・北の庄・白真弓
三千盛・磯自慢・若竹おんななかせ・初亀・満寿一・志太泉・葵天下・明眸
蓬来泉・初夢桜・若戎・神府・松の司・月の桂・招徳・玉乃光・秋鹿・呉春・天野酒
白鷹・倭小槌・小鼓・梅乃宿・春鹿・諏訪泉・豊の秋・李白・武蔵乃里・御前酒
賀茂泉・雨後の月・華鳩・富久長・誠鏡・旭菊水・五橋・金冠黒松・芳水・綾菊
金陵・梅錦・雪雀・京美人・酔鯨・司牡丹・土佐鶴・萬代・箱入娘・窓乃梅・香露
霊山・菊の城・千代の園・西の関・千羽鶴・角の井・その他全国の名酒を揃えて。

長谷川酒店
酒店
HASEGAWA LIQUORS SHOP
Liquor Shop
AD, D:Kensuke Irie

河本康孝
イラストレーション
Yasutaka Kawamoto
Illustration
AD, D, I:Yasutaka Kawamoto

国際酒会
酒協会
KOKUSAI SAKE KAI
Sake Association
AD:Ryo Urano
A, D:Dan Sato

仏蘭西菓子霧笛楼
レストラン
FRANCE KASHI MUTEKIRO
Restaurant
DF：Banwa Agency

すみや
和食店
SUMIYA
Japanese Restaurant
AD，D：Hiroshi Takahara

翁
和食店
OKINA
Japanese Restaurant
AD：Hiroshi Takahara
D：Eiko Nara

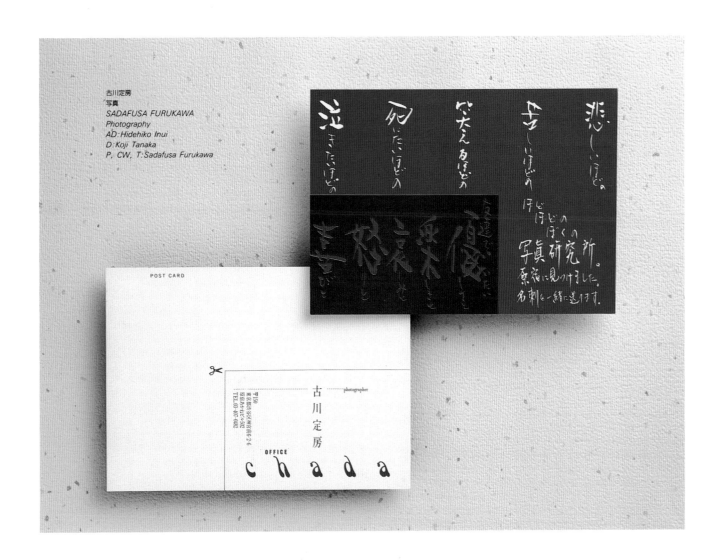

古川定房
写真
SADAFUSA FURUKAWA
Photography
AD:Hidehiko Inui
D:Koji Tanaka
P, CW, T:Sadafusa Furukawa

異風麦酒屋 東菜
レストラン/バー
IFUMUGIZAKAYA TOZAI
Restaurant/Bar
AD, D:Hiroki Taniguchi

城山ヤブ椿を楽しむ会
サークル
SIROYAMA-YABUTSUBAKI-O-TANOSIMU-KAI
Circle
AD:Tetsuya ota
I:Zenji Funabashi

かとうゆめこ
アーティスト
YUMEKO KATO
Artist
A:Yumeko Kato

有ゲコ・ショーケース
広告代理店
GECKO SHOWCASE
Advertising Agency
AD，D：Toshihiro Onimaru

代表取締役
相羽美樹

有限会社ケコ・ショーケース
〒150 東京都渋谷区宇田川町2-1 渋谷ホームズ617
Tel.03-476-4759

gecko showcase

gecko
showcase

gecko
showcase

有限会社
〒156 東
617 Shib
Shibuya-
Tel.03-4

g e c k o s h o w c a

有限会社ケコ・ショーケース
〒156 東京都渋谷区宇田川町2-1 渋谷ホームズ617
617 Shibuya Homes, 2-1 Udagawa-cho,
Shibuya-ku, Tokyo, 156 Japan.
Tel.03-476-4759

g e c k o s h o w c a s e